PEOPLE WHO KNEW JACK

as opposed to people who don't know jack

by

Jack Kenworthy

TELEMACHUS PRESS

This book is an autobiography. While the people, places, and events are real; some of the names and descriptions have been changed to protect individual privacy.

Cover designed by Telemachus Press, LLC

Cover art:
Copyright © iStockphoto/5735478/mcfields
Copyright © iStockphoto/13125421/jgareri

Interior photographs are the property of Jack Kenworthy

Published by Telemachus Press, LLC
http://www.telemachuspress.com

ISBN: 978-1-940745-95-4 (eBook)
ISBN: 978-1-940745-96-1 (Paperback)

Version 2014.06.03

Printed in the United States of America

10 9 8 7 6 5 4 3 2 1

Dedication

This endeavor is dedicated to the scores of people who knew Jack and are cited in this book ... and to the thousands of others who knew Jack who are not mentioned. I could have written another 400 pages of anecdotes about you. Thanks to all of you for enriching my life.

TABLE OF CONTENTS

PEOPLE WHO KNEW JACK

as opposed to people who don't know jack

INTRODUCTION

I INTRODUCED MYSELF to a contractor who was working on my back porch a few years ago. After we shook hands, he said to me, "I'm glad I met you, Jack. Now nobody can tell me that I don't know jack." That classic response was the inspiration for the title of this publication.

I have felt for some time that I should relate and record some of my experiences. Being actively involved with community college students for thirty years and with some interesting and funny senior citizens for an additional fifteen years, I felt that I had some stories to tell. I undertook this project, first for myself, as a way to organize my memoirs and make my life venture somewhat finite (note to self: I still hope to have many more years of living). Secondly, some of my family members and friends may find my story interesting. This writing endeavor has been a satisfying way for me to recall my life experiences with particular emphasis on all the people that I have known throughout my lifetime. As I look back over my 70-plus years, I have had some unique experiences, many of which contained some humor (my parents' legacy included an abundance of humor). I knew some interesting people, some of them were dynamic, some were mentors and very influential in my life, some were inspirational; and some were just funny and fun to be with. My legacy has been formed by a combination of my life's experiences and the many and varied people who have touched my life in some way or another.

If you conduct a Google search of Jack Kenworthy, you probably won't find many hits. I am not rich or famous. While I am proud of many of my accomplishments, these accomplishments are limited in comparison to those of so many other people. I have not made major strides in solving world peace. I have not participated in significant scientific research. I am not a renowned surgeon. I am not a noted business leader or statesman. On the few occasions that various agencies and services were closed down due to tropical storms or hurricanes in Brevard County and only "essential personnel" were told to report to work, I was always classified as "non-essential." While I consider myself somewhat wise with insightful "gut instincts" about many things, I am not particularly intelligent. While attending the University of Florida, I discovered that I had to devote many more hours of study and preparation than most of my more intelligent classmates. Having lived in Brevard County in east-central Florida for over 45 years, my name is recognizable to some residents of Brevard County. Staying active within several sports and fitness circles over the years, Jack is known to a limited number of people.

As a former athlete and coach, I considered myself better than average. I was not an All-American or "world class athlete," but I was pretty good. While not an All-American, I did manage to "walk-on" without a baseball scholarship at the University of Florida in Gainesville, Florida, and to subsequently receive a scholarship. I was named "All-Conference" for the Southeastern Conference as a catcher in my senior year of eligibility. I was also elected team captain my senior year. As a baseball coach at Brevard Community College, I felt that I was able to help many adolescents become better athletes, students, and responsible adults; but, I also feel that I failed to bring out the best in many of my athletes. As a coach, I won more games than I lost. Perhaps it can be said of me what was on the gravestone of a deceased baseball coach in Vermont: "All he asked was that he win his share of games." In addition to not being famous, I never possessed a lot of money, either. My wife, Gloria, and I had to pinch pennies and be creative to pay bills for a few decades. So, who cares about people who knew Jack? Anyone who lives long enough can put together an interesting life story, even if he is an ordinary, humble guy. I consider myself an ordinary, humble guy.

My father, Hugh (aka **Ken**), lived a good life for over 91 years. For many of those later years, I had thought about conducting interviews to "pick his brain" for all of his experiences. He was born in Wales, came to the United States at an early age to live in southeastern Massachusetts. He attended an agricultural school, aspired to be a chicken farmer, married **Lois**, struggled as the Great Depression began, worked in construction in Trinidad, worked in ship building, became a plumber, and completed his career in the civil service as a "planner and estimator" in Guantanamo Bay, Cuba. Throughout all of these experiences, "Ken" (as he was known by everyone) provided for four offspring—Joan, Hugh, Jr., Frank, and me. He retired and spent much of his time enjoying his 21 grandchildren and maintaining reasonably good health. He was married to Lois for 47 years, before she succumbed to cancer in 1976. A couple of years later, he married Marie Clough, and they were married for 20 years. Ken passed away in 1999, and Marie passed away a year or two later. That was his life in a nutshell; but, I wish I knew more of the details. He was an athlete himself, playing basketball for Bristol County Agriculture School; and, he coached basketball at that school. Somewhere, there are love letters when he was courting Lois. Somewhere there are accounting ledger books that showed that he "lost his a**" trying to become a young chicken farmer, as the Great Depression took its grip on this country. There are so many other details of Ken's life that I wish I had known. I wish I had taken the time to document the stories of Ken and Lois and their rich experiences. As a gift to my family, I am doing that on these pages.

In the year 2014, I am mostly retired from formal employment. I still have some structure in my life: I work part-time at a hospital-based fitness center; I keep the official scorebook for Florida Tech (a local Division II university) basketball; I try to keep our homes in Florida and Virginia reasonably maintained; I like to stay physically active, kayaking, bicycling, walking, playing handball, and occasionally jogging. I hope that my health allows me to continue to participate in these activities for many years.

At 70 years of age, I have some time to recall and reflect on my life. I also still maintain some of my memory (even if it is selective memory). While I try to be truthful, I can only go with the memory and perceptions that remain in my aging mind. Gloria, my wife, recently had her 50th high school reunion. One of her former classmates mentioned that he would like to reminisce, but he can't remember anything. I can't remember certain events and people in my life either. I also reserve the right to omit some of the ugly experiences. While some unpleasant things have occurred in my life, there haven't been many. I have looked at some of the trying times and turned them around as positive outcomes. My mother, Lois, influenced me by viewing life's events positively through rose-colored glasses. Ken and Lois would often find humor during trying times. People often reflect what lessons their parents taught them. The most valuable legacy to me from Ken and Lois was their sense of humor. Corny quips and sarcasm have been my strategy in dealing with problems and crises and keeping my sanity throughout this busy and stressful life.

In summary, I am writing this book primarily for my own satisfaction, secondly for some interested family members, and thirdly, for anyone else who may be interested in this unique story. I was inspired by a former journalist for a local newspaper who once told me that everyone has a story to tell.

THE SWANSEA YEARS

**A recent photo of our Milford Road home in Swansea.
We lived here until 1955.**

I WAS BORN in Fall River, Massachusetts on August 16, 1943. My given name is John Andrew Kenworthy. I remember Lois saying jokingly that my name was selected, because every house should have a "john" (meaning a bathroom facility). In my early years I was called Jackie. I lived my first 12 years on Milford Road in Swansea, Massachusetts. I still visit southeastern Massachusetts from time to time, and the house is still standing, although it is in a deteriorating state and looks as if it needs to be demolished. As an infant and child, I obviously remember little. Like most people, I was a "mama's boy" and spent most of my time around the house with my mother—no daycare. I suspect Ken was working hard as a plumber in the late 1940's, and did a lot of moonlighting to make ends meet. Working mothers and daycare facilities were rare in those days. From comments I can remember, I was spoiled by my mother, Lois. I was the youngest in the family by six years. Perhaps I was a mistake or an afterthought. In the two years prior to 1943, Ken was working in Trinidad, operating heavy equipment at a military camp in preparation for the outbreak of World War II. It is possible that my mother and father "missed each other" and upon Ken's return to the United States, I was the result of that long separation—a child of lust.

My sister, **Joan**, was 15 years older than me. She babysat me often, I suspect. I remember that she was a cheerleader at Case High School in Swansea and that she was musically inclined. I have a faded memory of Joan and me, and I am not proud of that event. A farmer's association called "the grange" was somewhat prevalent in Massachusetts in those days. The "Swansea Grange" was a social hall that was a venue for several events. One such event was a musical talent show. Joan, maybe 20, entered this show with her baby brother Jackie (me), maybe 5, and we were singing a duet. I don't remember what song we were singing, but I decided to stop singing that song and to start singing a popular song at the time that had lyrics "I don't want her—you can have her—she's too fat for me," as I pointed at Joan. Well, the audience laughed and loved it, and this 5-year old continued working the crowd until an embarrassed Joan pulled me off the stage. I apologized to Joan in later years, but I don't blame her if she didn't accept the apology.

Joan studied at the Boston Conservatory of Music for a couple of years, married **Tom Halloran**, and became a mother six times. Tom was handsome and a good singer. In his younger years, he could have been mistaken for Dean Martin, a popular singer at the time. On many occasions over the years, Joan would sit down at the piano and accompany Tom and other family members in sing-alongs. For many years, Joan was a music director for various churches.

Tom and Joan had a son and five daughters. Sadly, Tom passed away in 2011. Joan was diagnosed with some form of dementia in 2010. She could still tune in to some of her long-term memory, but became confused, trying to live life in the present. Joan passed away in 2014.

I never took up hunting and I was discouraged by Lois to shoot any weapons of any kind (as was my brother, Frank) as a child. The reason for Lois' aversion to shooting weapons was an experience that my brother, **Hugh, Jr**. had as a youngster. While playing with a neighbor boy, Hugh was accidentally shot in the eye with an arrow from a home-made bow and arrow set and lost sight in one eye. Lois would recall the horror of seeing her son coming to the house all bloody in the face. Hugh, Jr. went through life with one eye. He was a good high school football player. He even boxed for a while, until he took one too many punches coming from his blind spot.

I can remember one Thanksgiving morning when Case High School was playing its neighboring rival, Somerset, in the annual football game. Hugh was injured. He had taken a blow to the head, and was knocked out for a period of time. He was put on the team bus, while the game continued. Our mother, Lois, went over to the bus to check on her son's condition. As she approached Hugh, she heard a proliferation of obscenities coming out of his mouth. Lois was shocked. She had never heard her son use that kind of language before. Hugh didn't remember this event. Most likely Hugh suffered a concussion, but getting your bell rung in football was accepted more in the early 1950's than it is today. Hugh recovered and never used that kind of language around his mother again.

Hugh had a girlfriend at Case High School. Her name was **Irene Durand**, a petite and pretty product of a loud and fun-loving French-Canadian family. Hugh and Irene married in 1952. Gloria and I went to his 50th wedding celebration in 2002. What a celebration! Lots of video and photo presentations with many people relating their memories of Hugh and Irene. The event lasted for over four hours, and people couldn't get enough. Finally Hugh got to the podium to speak to a standing ovation. Hugh cited the few people in attendance, who were at the wedding 50 years ago. Hugh said he remembered them being there. He remembered the wedding, the reception, and driving away with Irene. Then he said, "The next 50 years were just a blur." I have not yet mentioned how large his family was.

All family members were asked to share any memories we had of Hugh and Irene at that 50th anniversary celebration. I put together a recollection of an event that occurred before they were married, and it went over pretty well. The script to that presentation follows:

DOUBLE-DATE AT THE SOMERSET DRIVE-IN
by Jack Kenworthy

I was the youngest of four children of Hugh, Sr. and Lois Kenworthy. Rumor had it that I was perhaps a "child of lust," having been conceived after my father (Hugh, Sr.) returned from Trinidad. That event made me about 10 years younger than Hugh, Jr.

Some time around 1950, Hugh, Jr. was dating Irene Durand. I was around 7 years old, and I suspect that somebody had to look after "Jackie" one night. I was told that I had an opportunity to go to the drive-in movie theater in Somerset with Hugh and Irene—and Irene's sister, Lorraine (a couple of years younger than Irene and 8 or 9 years older than me). That sounded like a good deal to me, and when we arrived, Lorraine and I were told that we had to sit in the front seat, while Hugh and Irene sat in the back seat. That sounded like a good deal also, since I could sit in front of the steering wheel and get a better view of the movie. I didn't understand why Hugh and Irene agreed to give up their great seats for the back seat at the time, but I think I understand now. I think that technically Lorraine was baby-sitting me. In subsequent years Lorraine became a nun. Even though she was baby-sitting, she was also technically my "date" that night. Guys are not proud of their "dates" eventually going into the convent.

Anyway, nothing happened in the front seat of that car, and I really don't know what happened in the back seat of the car, but I will always remember the night that Lorraine and I double-dated with Hugh and Irene at the Somerset Drive-In.

Irene was a Roman Catholic (a <u>good</u> Roman Catholic), and Hugh was not affiliated with any particular church at the time. They had 10 children and 34 grandchildren (and at least 40 great-grandchildren). Weddings and childbirths are constantly occurring, and there is no indication that they are going to stop occurring.

They lived their early years together in Rehoboth, Massachusetts. Hugh worked as a production line supervisor for a manufacturing company. In 1975 Hugh and Irene decided to sell everything they owned and move to

Tomah, Wisconsin to buy a small working dairy farm—with 10 kids and a couple of in-laws (a couple of the older kids were then married). Hugh's only experience as a dairy farmer in Massachusetts was the ownership of one cow, appropriately named "Necessity." In the early 1990's, Hugh and Irene succeeded in getting their family raised and married off. So, what did they do for an encore? Hugh sold all his cows, retired as a dairy farmer, and he and Irene joined the Peace Corps and spent 27 months in Ecuador.

Hugh and Irene spent much of their time in Wisconsin, attending weddings (of grandchildren) and trying to keep up with all the childbirths (of great-grandchildren). Much of their family still lives in Wisconsin. Hugh and Irene became active members of the Seventh Day Adventist Church. While their families have all the drama and crises that most families have, they have proved to be resilient and fun-loving. My assessment of what makes this family special is the genetic and sociological mix. Hugh was good hearted with a sense of humor (he got that from Ken and Lois), and Irene came from a family that talked a lot and laughed a lot. Their offspring have inherited those synergistic attributes. Attending their family weddings (there are usually 2 or 3 per year) is always a loud, fun, and uplifting experience.

Sadly, Hugh passed away in August of 2013 with cardiovascular issues. I always admired the way Hugh lived his life. For his final act, he died in style. In the last days of his life, he was too weak to get out of bed. He relied on a CPAP machine, a breathing apparatus that forces oxygen into the lungs. His doctor said that without the CPAP machine, he would die in a short period of time. His loving family determined that they could no longer care for him at home and made the decision to transfer him to a hospice facility. On his second night in the hospice facility, the last family member had left for the evening. The hospice nurse checked on Hugh in his weakened state unable to move at 7 p.m. When she returned to his room at 7:30, she found him dead. He had removed his CPAP mask and somehow gathered enough strength to get out of bed and face pictures of his huge family that were on the wall. He was found dead in the prayer position alongside the bed, facing the pictures. He died on his own terms. His funeral was held at his small Seventh Day Adventist Church in Tomah, Wisconsin. I questioned the choice of the small venue. He was very much loved and respected by family and friends, and many people would be attending his funeral service. The church was not nearly large enough to accommodate the multitude of attendees at the funeral. Hugh insisted that the funeral be held at the small church. He was an elder at the church and was known to have said to his pastor, "Wouldn't it be great, if we could fill up this church some day?" The church was jam-packed with many people forced to witness the service from the front lawn. To top it all off, he pulled off a spectacular feat. Hugh's daughter, Mary Beth (aka **"Maggie Mae"**), is a popular professional country singer particularly in the Midwest. One of her many released CD's included a rendition of the classic hymn "How Great Thou Art," featuring her dad, Hugh, as a soloist and her mother, Irene, on the piano. As his casket was leaving the church, that recorded song was being played, and he was singing the very moving hymn, accompanied by Irene. He had the opportunity to sing at his own funeral.

My brother, **Frank**, was six years older than me. With the fifteen-year, ten-year, and six-year differences in age; I didn't have a traditional sibling relationship with Joan, Hugh, and Frank. I was the "afterthought," essentially living life as an only child. Both Hugh and Frank were very good athletes at Case High School in Swansea, Massachusetts, and I aspired to be like them, playing sports at Case High School. Fate changed my athletic future.

Frank picked on his kid brother (me) often with frequent bruises (frogs) to the upper arm and other harassments. I think Frank and Hugh were instrumental in my batting left-handed. In the early fifties, the two premier hitters in major league baseball were Ted Williams of the Boston Red Sox and Stan Musial of the St. Louis Cardinals—both left-handed hitters. For that reason my brothers were determined to make me a left-handed batter. Also, I was reminded that left-handed batters are a half step closer to first base than right-handed batters, after they hit the ball. I have recollections of being told to pick up a bat and swing it; I would naturally bat right-handed. Then Frank would give me a frog in the upper arm and have me turn around to bat left-handed. After an armful of bruises, I decided that the path of least resistance would be to bat left-handed. As a young Little Leaguer, I would cry when I struck out, so I adapted my swing to more consistently make contact with the ball. In baseball coaching terms, my swing was "inside out" with a swing arc that increased my chances of making contact with the ball without swinging and missing. The coaching terms for my style of hitting were: "banjo hitter," "punch and judy hitter," or "cunnythump hitter" (as Dave Fuller, my college coach, would describe my batting style). When I was a senior at the University of Florida, Coach Fuller experimented with me hitting right-handed and assessed that I had a more traditional swing right-handed; but, by then it was too late to change.

At age 8 I felt most comfortable batting right-handed, but brothers Hugh and Frank insisted that I bat left-handed. Note the look of uncertainty with a right-handed hitter's stance and a left-handed hitter's grip.

Frank was instrumental in my first experience as a baseball player. Frank was 13, and I was 7. Frank was playing in a Swansea summer baseball league for teenagers under the direction of **Tony Aguiar**, a college student on summer break. I was tagging along and was on the sidelines doing whatever 7-year olds do while their older brother is playing baseball. Something controversial happened in the game, causing Frank to yell an expletive. Tony informed Frank that he was ejected from the game. There were no substitutes available, so Tony said, "Jackie, go play second base."

In the spring of 1955 I can remember watching a high school baseball game between Case and Somerset, Case's arch rival. Somerset had a huge lead in the top of the fifth inning, but black clouds were rolling in, threatening to cancel the game. The league rules were that the game would be cancelled, unless there were five full innings completed. If cancelled, the two teams would have to re-play the game from scratch on another day. Somerset decided that they needed to make the third out quickly to speed up the game to get five innings completed before the rains came. Conversely, Case wanted to stall the game, hoping for a rainout. Somerset had a man on second base with two outs. A ground ball was hit to Frank at third base. The base runner on second base decided he would run toward Frank, so he could get tagged out to speed up the game. As the runner was approaching Frank, my brother dropped the ball and glove and executed a cross body block at the runner. The benches emptied, and a brawl ensued. The rains came, and the game was cancelled. My brother was a hero (in some people's eyes). The game was re-played the next day, at which time Somerset won by a large margin.

In the fall of 1955 I was attending Case Junior High School for a few days before I was leaving Swansea and leaving the country (more about that later). During roll calls in class, I noticed many long looks and strange facial expressions when teachers read the name "Jack Kenworthy." Frank was starting his senior year at Case High School, so he must have left an impression (maybe positive-maybe negative) with many of the faculty members. I perceived that he often stayed in trouble with those in authority at Case High. He referred to himself as the black sheep of the family. He married **Nancy Grime** from arch rival Somerset, moved to Miami, Florida and had two daughters, Wendy and Cindy. Ironically, Nancy's father, Chick Grime, was a good friend of our father, Ken, during their younger years.

When I was young, Frank bullied me some; but, I accepted that bullying was what older brothers did to kid brothers. I recovered from all the bruises on the arm. Frank excelled in football and baseball, and I was proud of his accomplishments. I idolized him—even if he had the reputation of bad boy.

Frank was helpful to me in many ways during our adult years, since we were both Floridians. Frank lives in Miramar, Florida. He is semi-retired with a plumbing firm. Frank and Nancy divorced in 1976. Many suspect that because Frank and Nancy had so much respect for Lois, they did not divorce until Lois passed away.

In addition to my parents and my siblings, there was one additional resident in our Milford Road home. Emma Biltcliffe was my mother's aunt. She was widowed decades before. Her father was Andrew Townley, who was a Civil War veteran for the Union Army and died a couple of years after the conclusion of the war. In the early 1950's she was approaching her nineties. She was temperamental and opinionated, which meant that she was difficult to live with. I witnessed on several occasions her throwing playing cards in frustration and disgust, while playing bridge at our dining room table. Emma Biltcliffe was affectionately known as "**Auntie Bill.**" The story was told that Auntie Bill's health took a severe turn in 1938, and that she allegedly had only a few months to live. Lois talked Ken into letting her live with them on Milford Road in Swansea. She arrived at our Milford Road home in 1938 and stayed with us until she passed away in 1954. I perceived that Ken bore the brunt, burden, and harassment of Auntie Bill's wrath. Auntie Bill's favorite was my brother, Hugh. He received preferential treatment and could do no wrong in her mind. Ken, Joan, Frank, and I did not feel the same love that Hugh received from Auntie Bill. I can remember hearing Auntie Bill say to Lois that she and Ken should have never had me. In later years, others told me that Auntie Bill referred to me as a "child of lust."

I always associate the word "physic," which is an archaic term for laxative, with Auntie Bill. As a young child, when I would be irritable, I can remember Auntie Bill telling Lois that I needed a "physic." I never heard that word used in that context ever again.

My parents were members of Christ Episcopal Church in Swansea, a beautiful stone structure in the bucolic, historic section of town called Swansea Village. My parents and Joan were active members; Hugh and Frank were not. I sang in a children's choir and attended Sunday school.

As a child I considered Episcopal priests to be saintly, righteous, holy, pompous, and worshipful. I can remember one Sunday night when there was a knock on our door. Someone looked out the window and announced that it was **Father Smith**. Panic ensued, because there was a game of bridge being played on the dining room table; and, good Episcopalians did not play cards on the Lord's Day. Frantically the Kenworthys made the cards disappear and removed any evidence of a bridge game before letting Father Smith in the house.

In the early 1950's a new priest came to Christ Church. **Father Francis Glazebrook** had a priestly, Anglican name; but, he didn't act the part. He was a young, dynamic, and athletic (which got my attention) Princeton graduate, who organized ice hockey games on Milford Pond, which was not far from our Milford Road home. What a neat guy he was!— a priest who played hockey! About that time (1951) Swansea was initiating little league baseball. Father Glazebrook became a little league coach. He made it a priority to identify all of the Episcopalian kids in the town of Swansea. As a result, he drafted all those Episcopalian kids to be on his team. The Swansea Little League Giants roster was 80% Episcopalian (including me). Father Glazebrook moved on to a church in New Hampshire a few years later, and we later learned that he died in an automobile accident there. He was a likeable clergyman, and he inspired me at a young age.

At 8 years-old, I was the youngest baseball player in the Swansea Little League; which in its infancy did not have a minor division, nor a machine-pitch division, nor a tee-ball division for the lesser skilled or younger play-ers. The Giants were pretty good, however they got better in the ensuing years. Father Glazebrook stepped down as the Giants coach after that first year and yielded to **Dick Enos**. I remember Dick as someone in his late 20's or early 30's—a driven coach, who brought out the best in his young athletes. Father Glazebrook's emphases were to have fun playing baseball and to keep Swansea's Episcopalian kids off the streets and out of trouble. Dick taught and coached baseball skills and instilled competitiveness in his players. The Giants responded and were consistently among the best teams in the Swansea Little League during the summers of 1953-54-55. I mostly played catcher for those teams. Catching was attractive to me; because, the catcher was in the middle of all the action with no chance of getting bored or distracted, as opposed to playing most of the other positions. In just a few years Dick Enos would pass away. One of his legs was atrophied, and he walked with a severe limp. I believe that his crippled condition was congenital. Walking with the limp caused excessive stress to his spinal cord and led to his deteriorating health, resulting in his demise. Dick Enos was instrumental in my early development as a young baseball player.

In the early 1950's I was enthralled by sports. I played Little League baseball. I played an abundance of "pick-up" sandlot baseball games (which Dick Enos despised, because he didn't want his players showing up tired for our early-evening Little League games). I played in youth basketball leagues. I attended Case High School athletic events, watching Hugh and Frank play various sports. I idolized my brothers, Hugh and Frank, because they were both very good high school athletes. My primary aspiration was to be a multi-sport athlete at Case High School. But, that never happened.

My siblings in Wisconsin in 2007. From left to right: Jack, Frank, Hugh, and Joan.

GTMO

KEN WAS THE sole provider in our family. He worked hard to put food on the table at our Milford Road home in Swansea. He did a lot of moonlighting to extend his limited income. In the early 1950's he had a job in Davisville, Rhode Island—one of the better paying jobs in his lifetime up to that time. Ken was laid off in 1954. As a kid, I perceived stress, dejection, gloom, and depression around our household—not to mention less food on the dinner table and less money available for clothes or movies or anything fun. Ken desperately looked for any employment he could find. He searched some publications that featured overseas jobs and submitted several applications for employment, remembering his experience working construction in Trinidad in 1941. Many months went by with no responses. Then a response came for a civil service job in a place called Guantanamo Bay Naval Base in Cuba. Ken accepted the job offer, thinking that he would have to leave his family behind while he worked in the Caribbean. After arriving in GTMO (military acronym for Guantanamo Bay) in early 1955, he learned that there were accommodations for him to have his family join him in Cuba. A few months later Lois and I were heading to New York City to take a military ship from the Brooklyn Navy Yard to Guantanamo Bay, Cuba.

Guantanamo Bay is located in the extreme southeast corner of the island of Cuba. The naval base, which consisted of 45 square miles of land and water, was acquired through a lease agreement with Cuba after the Spanish-American War in 1903. Its initial purpose was to be a fueling station for ships going through the Panama Canal. When World War II broke out, GTMO assumed various war-time functions. After World War II, GTMO was utilized as a training facility for the U.S. Navy, hosting various Sixth Fleet Navy ships as they would take training cruises throughout the Caribbean Sea. GTMO was serving this function, when Ken, Lois, and I arrived in 1955. In later years GTMO would serve as a place to temporarily house Cubans and Haitians, after they were captured by the U.S. Coast Guard. They were attempting to flee their respective countries intent on arriving on United States soil. In more recent years GTMO was best known as the site of a prison for world-wide terrorists.

The cruise to GTMO aboard the military transport ship setting sail from the Brooklyn Navy Yard lasted a few days. I remember the cruise for the very tasty food during every meal. I also remember meeting a Tennessee boy my age, who informed me that I talked funny. Having never been out of New England all 12 years of my existence, I had never been told by anyone that I talked with an accent. He was the one who talked funny. I was offended. We arrived at GTMO on a Sunday morning and were escorted directly to the chapel for Protestant services and Sunday school.

I subsequently learned that a military transport ship arrived every other Sunday morning and that the families were coerced to go directly to the chapel after they disembarked. As I learned to appreciate the opposite sex, I realized you could check out the new girls arriving in GTMO by attending church regularly (or at least every other Sunday). This gave you an advantage of being the first to scout the newly-arriving cute girls. There were no specific church denominations—just Protestants (I guess any Christians who are not Catholic) and Roman Catholics. The chapel had a rotating altar, so both factions used the same church building.

I was not too happy about being in GTMO. I didn't appreciate leaving Swansea. Brother Frank was able to stay in Swansea to finish his senior year. I missed all my friends. I wanted to watch Case High School athletics, and I wanted to be a future Case athlete. My mother and father were aware that I was not happy, but GTMO was where the work was, and I had to deal with it.

The lifestyle of a teenager in GTMO was totally different from my Swansea experiences. Kids came from all over the country, although a predominance of them had lived at least some of their life in the Norfolk, Virginia area, since Norfolk was the hub of the Navy's Sixth Fleet. Living on a military base meant that sociologically there was a defined caste system. Some kids' parents had Officers' Club privileges, which meant that they could use Officers' Club facilities (like swimming pool and restaurant). They were considered in the upper echelon of the social stratum, i.e., they were more "cool" and "privileged" in some people's eyes. Dependents of enlisted men (active duty servicemen receiving the lower pay scale and rank) had their own facilities, but were not able to benefit from any of the officers' privileges. This social dynamic was ever present and had the potential to restrict certain friendships or create awkward situations. Ken and Lois informed me that I didn't have Officers' Club privileges, which disturbed me. For some reason, we did acquire Officers' Club privileges after being on the base three years. I had a good mix of friends of the "not-so-privileged" and the "privileged."

A popular activity for teenagers on the base was to ride the bus. Navy gray buses traveled throughout the base from 7 am to 11 pm. If you had nothing better to do, you could ride the bus at no cost throughout the base—sometimes two or three circuits. The bus traveled from all the housing areas on the base to the Navy Exchange (the only substantial retail store), to the Commissary (the food market), to the Naval Station, to the Naval Air Station, down by the ship docks, to Public Works (where Ken worked), to the Marine barracks, to the hospital, and back to the housing areas. Each circuit took over an hour and a half, and you just hoped that some of your friends would eventually get on the bus.

Another popular activity for teenagers was the Teenage Club, which consisted of a Quonset hut and an attached patio. We had dances on weekend nights there. There were table tennis, board games, a juke box, and a short-order canteen that served soft drinks, hamburgers, and ice cream. The Teenage Club served as the place to hang out for all of us, regardless of our parents' status as officers or enlisted men.

There were free first-run movies at five different locations on the base. Movies were shown each night, and I was one of the lucky kids, whose parents would let him attend the movies even on week nights. I think that Ken and Lois realized that I resented having to leave Swansea and let me go out on week nights, as long as I kept my grades up (which I did). Another factor was that I was the fourth of their four kids; which meant that they were "burned out parents," and I was spoiled.

I learned to play golf on a course that had barren fairways. Golfers were allowed to bring their own Astroturf mats on the course. The rules permitted them to lay their mats in the fairway and place the golf ball on the mat in order to hit it. Ken and Lois were avid golfers.

We enjoyed the clear Caribbean waters. I did a little snorkeling and spear fishing with a really dangerous spear gun. I feel lucky that I didn't injure or kill anyone (including me), while fiddling with those elastic bungee cords to "load" the spear gun. We enjoyed renting cabanas at Windmill Beach and cooking out and swimming in the Caribbean, but wearing shoes was mandatory, because of the presence of sharp and dangerous coral. There were no sandy beaches in GTMO—just rocks and coral, but once you got into the water with your goggles on, the underwater scenery was beautiful with colorful fish and coral formations.

Jack, Lois, and Ken departing for Miami in 1956 from the Guantanamo City Airport. I remember seeing sugar cane fields on both sides of the runway

I attended William T. Sampson Junior and Senior High School, an American school for dependants of active-duty servicemen and civil service employees on the base. I participated in student government, acted in school plays, and most importantly played basketball, softball, flag football, and participated in track and field activities. Since the school's student body was small in number, everybody was involved in many activities.

Three of my classmates at Sampson High made national and international news. **Chuck Ryan** was the ringleader of the three; he was nineteen in 1957 (a few years older than me) and was a junior in high school. He wore his black hair greasy and slicked back, similar to the hairstyle worn by "Fonzie" on the once popular television show, "Happy Days." Chuck lived in the same neighborhood as me, so we got to know each other. Just like "Fonzie," he was considered a bad boy. The other two classmates were **Vic Buehlman**, 17, and **Mike Garvey**, 15. In early 1957 they would travel off the base to a couple of nearby Cuban towns during the weekends. They made friends with some Cubans who were sympathetic to the leader of the Cuban rebel cause, Fidel Castro. Fidel had formed a guerrilla army called the "Army of the 26th de Julio." The army wore red and black armbands and operated in the mountains in southern Cuba not far from GTMO. They would wreak havoc on the government troops of Cuban dictator, Fulgencio Batista. One weekend the trio went off the base and didn't return. They had run away to join Castro's army. Fidel took advantage of the potential for international recognition and publicity by making arrangements for a Life Magazine crew to travel into the mountains to report on and photograph the three newest recruits to his rebel army.

Meanwhile, back in GTMO the fathers of Chuck, Vic, and Mike were disciplined harshly. Their military careers were severely marred. The military code stresses that personnel are responsible for the actions of their dependents. The military frowned on kids running away from home to join the rebel army in Cuba. Vic and Mike returned in a few weeks and were gone. Chuck returned to the base five months later by hitching a ride from Cuba onto the base aboard the "banana boat," operated by a Cuban vendor who sold fresh fruit and vegetables to GTMO residents. I was the first person that Chuck recognized upon his illegal return to the base. He asked me to escort him to Sampson High School, so he could see **Mr. Truman**

Scarborough, the school system superintendent. I escorted him to Mr. Scarborough's office to tell him a visitor was there to see him, and I never saw Chuck again until he appeared at a GTMO reunion in 1999. I assume Mr. Scarborough facilitated Chuck's surrendering himself to the authorities (Chuck passed away in 2012).

Throughout the late 1950's there were hostile engagements between Castro's rebel army and Batista's government troops not far from GTMO. We could often hear gunfire many miles away from our duplex apartment in GTMO. Even though the situation in Cuba was unstable, we were still able to travel through the northeast gate into Cuba, until Fidel decided to pull off another publicity stunt. "Liberty buses" would regularly transport sailors and marines off the base to nearby Guantanamo City, where they would get drunk, visit with prostitutes, and do whatever else sailors and marines do when they are on liberty. On many occasions I can remember seeing the packed buses leaving for Guantanamo City in the afternoon, returning several hours later with the passengers in a very loud and drunken state. The returning bus trip was a comical sight.

One night, members of Fidel's rebel army decided to hijack a bus full of drunken sailors and marines. The bus was driven into the mountains outside of Santiago, Cuba, and the servicemen were detained for a couple of days. At first, it appeared that this action would develop into a serious international diplomatic standoff. It soon became apparent that Fidel was only seeking international recognition for his rebel cause against Batista. The servicemen were treated humanely, and within forty-eight hours they were being returned unharmed to the base via U.S. Navy helicopters. One enlisted man, who was hijacked, had some explaining to do. It seems that three days before, he had left his apartment with his bowling bag, telling his wife that he was going bowling after work at the base bowling alley. Instead, he ended up in the Sierra Maestra mountains outside of Santiago, Cuba.

My grades in high school were pretty good, and there was discussion of the possibility of my going to college. My sister Joan studied music for a year or two after high school. Hugh and Frank never pursued college after high school. Ken's income limited any hope for any of them to go to college, but Ken landed on his feet when he acquired his job in

GTMO. His employment entitled him and his family to two free round trips to the states each year. Our two-bedroom, one bath duplex apartment cost him very little per month. I suspect that medical care was free. Booze was cheap. Golf was cheap. Bingo was cheap. Movies were free. Ken and Lois were accumulating more savings than they ever had in their life together.

When I think of my athletic life at GTMO, the person who stands out most prominently is **Coach Les West**. Coach West was a tall, gangly Texan from Waco, who was a physical education teacher, basketball coach, and in later years was the principal at Sampson High School. Everyone at Sampson was fond of Coach West, not just the kids who played basketball for him. He was the principal in October of 1962, when all the dependents on the base were evacuated during the historic Cuban missile crisis. I was in college by then, but some of my younger schoolmates told me how he was intent on reassuring the nervous student body that they were to get on the school buses and go to their homes, where they would be leaving GTMO within hours. He was a steadying force among many, who feared that World War III was imminent.

Sampson High School alumni have organized several reunions in the subsequent decades since then, and Coach West has attended some of them. He was the premier attendee at those reunions. I perceived him as a disciplinarian who subtly displayed a love and concern for his students and athletes while displaying a respect for the educational process.

One of the sports that Sampson High participated in was basketball. We played in the basketball league on the base, competing against military personnel, who ranged in age from 19 to 45. Our school team consisted of kids ranging in age from 13 to 17. To compensate for this maturity and talent discrepancy, the high school physical education teacher was allowed to play on the team. Coach West was a pretty good basketball player, being tall with bony elbows. We lost most of our games, but on occasion Coach would help us be competitive. I can remember on numerous times when we would meet at half-time and Coach West was not playing well, his favorite saying was, "I couldn't hit a bull in the ass with a bass fiddle," referring to his inaccurate shooting. I cherish all that I learned from Coach West, and I think that he was instrumental in my subsequent teaching and coaching career.

If I had to select a best friend from my high school years, it would have to be **Jim Weeks**. Jim came to GTMO during the summer before my junior year. Jim was a year older than me and was coming to GTMO for his senior year from Norfolk, Virginia. His dad was a civilian accountant, working for the Navy. Jim played basketball. We did somewhat daring and dangerous things together. We double-dated. We were each other's best buddy.

During the winter of 1960, Life Magazine sent some reporters and photographers to GTMO to do a spread on life at Guantanamo Bay. Fidel Castro had successfully overthrown Fulgencio Batista a year earlier as the leader of Cuba. Castro, representing the common people, had conducted his rebellious conflict against Batista, and he was very popular with the Cuban people. Six months after Fidel took control of Cuba, there were rumblings that he was developing a political relationship with the Communist USSR. Life Magazine was in GTMO to portray our lifestyle on the base, as international tension was simmering just a few miles from the base. Somehow (I don't remember how) Jim and I (two high school kids) ended up at a party of adults, which included two members of the visiting Life Magazine staff. We were introduced to them. I haven't mentioned that Jim was an eloquent speaker with a silver tongue, i.e., a good bullsh***er. Jim told the journalists that he and I were going to be playing in a basketball game the next day. Normally we played against military personnel, but arrangements were made for us to play an exhibition game against a Cuban high school team from neighboring Guantanamo City. The game would be played at an outdoor basketball court on the base. There were no indoor gymnasiums in GTMO at the time. Jim suggested that Life Magazine should attend this game; he even told them his uniform number and my uniform number. They showed up the next day, and several weeks later Life Magazine came out with an eight-page pictorial feature with an action photo that included Jim and me at that game.

INTERNATIONAL GAME pits basketball team from base high school (white shirts) against Cubans from Guantánamo City school. Americans won 54 to 12.

This photo appeared in a 1960 Life Magazine. My buddy, Jim Weeks (#15), was instrumental in getting this picture in the magazine. I (#25) appear to be posing for the photographer.

Jim graduated in June of 1960, and was accepted to the University of Florida in Gainesville. Jim would send me letters and pictures of life on the campus of the University of Florida, as I was finishing up my senior year at Sampson High. I subsequently attended the University of Florida a year later, and Jim was my mentor, helping me to adjust to college life. Adjustment was not easy; I had to transition from a high school graduating class of 8 to a freshman class of 2,400. I depended on Jim to ease this transition.

Fast-forwarding a year, during my freshman year and Jim's sophomore year at UF, Jim was in a quandary. Christmas break was approaching, and he had nowhere to go for Christmas. His dad had changed jobs, and his parents were now living in Guam. Going to Guam for Christmas was out of the question. I had arranged to go to Cecil Field Naval Air Station, which was near Jacksonville, to spend Thanksgiving with some friends, who formerly went to Sampson High with me in GTMO. My friends' dad was a Captain in the Navy, who had been transferred from GTMO to Cecil Field. Since Jim had nowhere to go on Thanksgiving either, I arranged for him to get invited to Jacksonville with me.

While we were in Jacksonville, Jim let it be known to the Navy Captain that he had nowhere to go for Christmas, and wouldn't it be great if he could go back to GTMO with Jack (me) for Christmas break? My plans for Christmas were to take a commercial plane to Norfolk, Virginia and to take a Military Air Transport plane to GTMO and back. The Captain said if he wore a military uniform, he might be able to get Jim on a plane from Jacksonville Naval Air Station to GTMO. Jim suggested he could wear his Air Force ROTC uniform. The Captain said that might work. He got Jim's mailing address in Gainesville and said he would send him an official-looking letter to present at the main gate to Jacksonville Naval Air Station. The Captain said he couldn't guarantee passage to GTMO, but he would see what he could do.

For Christmas vacation three weeks later, Jim and I caught a ride to Jacksonville with a friend. We dropped off Jim at the Jacksonville Naval Air Station in his Air Force ROTC uniform with his "official-looking" letter. I told him, "maybe I'll see you in a day or two," and I was driven to the Jacksonville Airport to catch a flight to Norfolk and then a Navy plane to GTMO (the traditional way for a dependent to fly into GTMO). Jim had still not appeared on the base the day after I arrived in GTMO. We had no way of communicating. Remember, we didn't have cell phones, texting capabilities, or email in 1961. While I was driving my father's car somewhere, a bus passed by with a guy in an Air Force ROTC uniform hanging out of an open window and yelling to me. I drove Jim to our house. I thought that my mother would be glad to see Jim; and, she was, until I informed her that he was going to stay at our house over the holiday break. She didn't appreciate all that Jim had done to get himself on the base. All she understood was that we would be harboring an illegal person at our house for a few days, and Ken would get in trouble with the Navy for this and could subsequently lose his job in GTMO. As a responsible adult now, I understand Lois' concerns, but in 1961 as an 18-year old, I thought that she was being a "spoil sport." Somehow I convinced her to allow Jim to stay at our house.

Jim and I had a great time the next few days and nights. Some of our Sampson High School friends had returned from college to GTMO for the holiday break, and people were hosting parties every night. Reality set in somewhere around January 2. Jim had talked his way onto the base; now he had to talk his way back to the states. He went to the Administration Building to explain his situation. He was referred to the base legal officer. The legal officer was pulling his hair out. "Why would anyone want to come to GTMO for Christmas vacation?" he asked. Several phone calls later Jim was told to keep his mouth shut about what he had done and to never come back to GTMO for any more vacations. He flew back to Jacksonville NAS the next day—in his Air Force ROTC uniform.

Jim graduated from the University of Florida with a degree in communications in 1965. His first job was in advertising sales with the Gainesville Sun, which was subsequently acquired by the New York Times. His whole career was affiliated with the New York Times, and he was successful. His last assignment was as President of the Southeast Region of the New York Times Newspaper Group. He had a nice home in a prestigious neighborhood in Atlanta. In late 2006 I felt lucky to have an opportunity to introduce my son, Russ, and my daughter, Shannon, to my old high school and college buddy. Two months later I received a phone call, informing me that Jim had passed away. The next day I received a call from Todd Weeks, his son. He said that his dad had always talked about his antics and other good times at GTMO and at the University of Florida, and he asked me if I would speak at his memorial service and recall some of our experiences together in high school and college. Speaking at a memorial service was new to me, but I was honored that he asked and drove to Atlanta the next day. I did have to "cull out" most of our experiences together during my tribute to Jim at his memorial service.

Going back to August of 1960, I was beginning my senior year at Sampson High School in a senior class of eight people. Jim was in Gainesville, Florida, beginning his college career and writing letters to me, giving me some insights of college life. My grades had been decent, and I was investigating some potential colleges for the next year. I sent requests for college catalogs to dozens of colleges. I narrowed my choices to Dartmouth College and the University of Florida. Tension built while awaiting acceptance/rejection letters from those two institutions. I don't know why Dartmouth was my first choice, but it was. I still longed to go back to New England; I still resented not going to Case High for my high school years. The Dartmouth rejection letter arrived, and while I was crushed, Ken was elated. Dartmouth was going to be expensive. I was accepted by the University of Florida (not as expensive). People were saying that Jack was going to experience going from being a big fish in a little pond to being a little fish in a gigantic pond. I was getting excited and apprehensive at the same time.

I played my fifth year of basketball for the high school team. I was a class president. I was a participant in a school play. I was pretty much a "big shot" in GTMO. I dated some of the good-looking girls. Dates consisted of going to the movies, going to the Teenage Club, and trying to find places to "make out" without getting caught by parents or the "base patrol."

Being the Valedictorian of a high school senior class gives you an elite status, and yes, I was the Valedictorian (of a class of eight). Even though the small class size takes some of the glisten away, I was and am still proud of my accomplishment. **Susan Tracy**, one of my nieces, called me in 2011 to say that she had discovered my Valedictorian speech in my sister Joan's attic, composed on 3x5 cards. I am including the speech below, because it reflects the hopes and fears of a goofy and naive 17-year older (me), who went to school on a sheltered military base during some very tense years of the Cold War:

Valedictorian Speech
William T. Sampson High School
June 1961

Rear Admiral O'Donnell
Mr. Murphy

Mr. West
And Friends

This is a Commencement Exercise. Many students consider it the finale to all those long and irritating homework assignments or to those never-ending days in school. After twelve years of schooling, we seniors look at a commencement exercise from a different standpoint. After all, the word "commencement" does not mean the end. In a few weeks all of us seniors will be experiencing a different way of life—we shall begin a new era of our lives.

Most of us will be attending college next year. One goes to college to study, to learn, and to obtain a degree with a business-like attitude. College is a business. Education is not free for me anymore. A college education costs a great amount of money, and it will cost even more money in the next few years. In other words, next year we seniors will be buying our education. Whether we get our money's worth or not depends on how much we choose to work.

Also, in a few weeks my classmates and I shall be passing through the portals to the land of adulthood. We shall be choosing our own careers and earning our own money. Adulthood and responsibility go hand-in-hand, especially when matrimony enters our lives. Then, before we know it, we'll be raising children ourselves, just as you have been doing. Yes parents, your little boys and girls will soon be making payments on their own: homes, automobiles, washing machines, stoves, freezers, and television sets. And perhaps if you live close enough to us, we'll be asking you to help us fill out our income tax forms.

Living under the Navy, most of us Guantanamo Bay teenagers are more dependent on our fathers than our counterparts in civilian life in the states. Everything is done through Dad or through Dad's command. This has been as true for the Class of '61, as for any other students here in GTMO. Even in matters touching our behavior, our parents are held more accountable than stateside parents usually are. If a youth acts mischievous, it is Dad's fault. True, this sense of dependency may be a great handicap to us, as we begin our adult life; but, when we take the big step into this complex world, we'll find our first challenge awaiting us.

But what kind of world are we entering? A world where practically all nations and all people are being constantly threatened by war. A place where two great world powers have the ability to destroy practically all civilization. The U.S. is in great danger of falling into the hands of the rapidly advancing Communists. Because of the Russians' ability to infiltrate less-developed countries, the U.S. is losing its respect and prestige more and more every day. At the present rate, our nation may soon be second best to a group of tyrants.

The youths of today realize this grave situation. We will stand by democracy, maintain democracy, and fight for democracy. There are many challenges confronting the U.S. and its principles. In the next decade or so, we teenagers may be called on to keep peace. We will have to keep America strong by making it stronger. Today's youth will also be striving to retain world leadership for the U.S., so that more countries may someday enjoy freedom.

Senator Humphrey from Minnesota recently stated, "What is needed today is a sense of urgency." This means that all of us, not just some politicians, have to meet all the United States' challenges with a more serious and conscientious attitude. If this sense of urgency can be acquired now, our job will certainly be much easier in the future.

I understand that the adults of today feel insecure and unsure about us teenagers. People criticize the way we are being educated. Well I am quite sure that our schools today have improved from the time when you went to school. Educators have learned (through mistakes and experience) which are the best methods of teaching today's youth. Students have greater opportunities to attend college now than you ever had.

If you are worried about our attitude toward national security, think about the many famous leaders and devoted workers of today, who survived the "Roaring Twenties." Yes, parents and friends, we shall survive also. In our own small graduating class there are potential leaders. Above all, though, we are devoted and conscientious students, who will definitely become informed U.S. citizens and loyal hard workers. We assure you that we will do our best in making our nation more powerful and more stable.

It has certainly been a pleasure being a member of the class of 1961. At the risk of sounding conceited, I want to say that I believe our class may go down in history as one of the best-behaved and hardest-working classes at Sampson High. Many adults have spoken of the senior class of 1961 in a very complimentary tone. Perhaps because our class was so small, we learned to work together well and became better friends because of it. Certainly we each had to work harder than we would have, if we had been a larger group.

Speaking for my class, I would like to say farewell to William T. Sampson, which has been a second home to many of us for two or three years. The dependence and irresponsibility of living on a Navy base will soon come to a close. Living in GTMO for more than three years, one may see many fine people come and go. We must say good-bye to all those wonderful friends we have encountered during our stay here on the Navy base. Our home life will be coming to a close, as soon as we begin our new ventures. This is one thing we will all miss. Perhaps when we return home from college on our Christmas vacation, we will learn to appreciate our homes even more.

Despite all the great changes coming up for us, there is one thing we can be sure of. God has guided us through our first eighteen years. He will not desert us now. No matter what happens to any of us, God will always be reigning to guide us, to strengthen us, and to inspire us. The first verse of Psalm 46 says, "God is our refuge and strength, a very present help in trouble; therefore, we will not fear though the earth should change." (End of Commencement Address)

I spent the summer of 1961 in GTMO, working for the Transportation Department, filing, doing courier-type work and other relatively meaningless tasks. All my co-workers were Cuban, and I had to step up my Spanish, in order to communicate. In the evenings I played baseball in the Navy League. Normally, the league was restricted to active-duty military personnel. Some people made it possible for a couple of us graduating seniors to participate in that league that summer. We were assigned to the Hospital team, consisting mostly of corpsmen (medics). I was the catcher, and I felt that I benefitted from playing among more skilled, more mature, and more experienced baseball players. I had a pretty good season as the catcher for the Hospital team, and it was appearing that baseball was the sport that showed the most athletic potential for me. I was determined to inquire about trying out for baseball at the University of Florida, when I arrived in Gainesville in September. At the conclusion of the Navy League season, I was pleasantly and proudly surprised to learn that I was voted the "Most Valuable Player" of the league, since I was the young kid playing in a league with active duty military personnel up to 50 years old. I still cherish that trophy proudly.

Ken and Lois would park their car down the right-field line to watch me play that summer. On one particular night Lois had left the car to go to the concession stand. In the area of the concession stand there was a paved path that led from the liberty boat landing to the E.M. (Enlisted Men's) Club, which was the "watering hole" for sailors and marines. Every night there would be a steady flow of very drunk sailors and marines, traversing from the E.M. Club to the liberty boat landing to return to their ships that were anchored out in the bay. At the E.M. Club a few dozen sailors had cornered a few marines, and a fight broke out on this night. Eventually, the out-numbered marines escaped and went to the landing to secure more marines as reinforcements. From the baseball field, we players could sense some commotion on that paved path. From his car down the right-field line, Ken was a little concerned. He left the car to search for Lois, and he found her near the paved path. About thirty drunken marines were coming from the landing. About thirty drunken sailors were approaching from the E.M. Club. A serious "rumble" was ensuing, and Lois was in the middle of about sixty drunks, trying to urge them to go home and sleep it off. Ken rescued Lois, and the Shore Patrol eventually restored order.

Lois was always attempting to be the peace-keeper. By that time, she had been on the base for six years, and she was a legend. She was loved and respected by many people. She was very sociable. Many people in GTMO regarded Lois as their mother-figure or grandmother-figure. She bowled; she golfed; she played bridge; she played bingo; she volunteered at the hospital; she counseled younger people through their problems. Lois just wanted everybody to get along and approached life from the positive side. Countless people would tell me how lucky I was to have her as a mother, and I had to agree with them. Since I was still a teenager, Lois and I had our conflicts, but I recognized how lucky I was to have a mother like Lois.

Before I left GTMO for the University of Florida that summer, a GTMO resident said he was going to write a letter of recommendation to the Gators basketball coach, recommending me as a basketball prospect. I didn't think I was that good at basketball, and I recognized that in GTMO I was a big fish in a little pond. I was heading to Gainesville, where I would be an insignificant minnow.

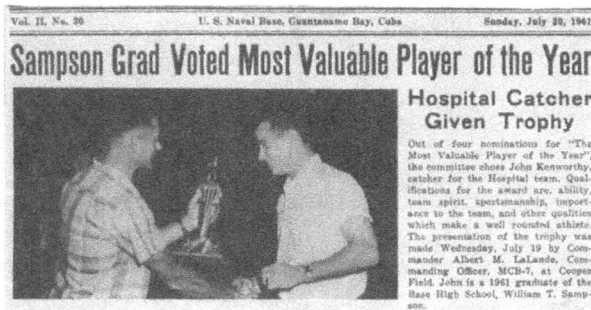

Vol. II, No. 20   U. S. Naval Base, Guantanamo Bay, Cuba   Sunday, July 30, 1961

Sampson Grad Voted Most Valuable Player of the Year

Hospital Catcher Given Trophy

Out of four nominations for "The Most Valuable Player of the Year", the committee chose John Kenworthy, catcher for the Hospital team. Qualifications for the award are, ability, team spirit, sportsmanship, importance to the team, and other qualities which make a well rounded athlete. The presentation of the trophy was made Wednesday, July 19 by Commander Albert M. LaLande, Commanding Officer, MCB-7, at Cooper Field. John is a 1961 graduate of the Base High School, William T. Sampson.

I never saw this award coming, but I am proud of it. I was the youngest player in the league, which was comprised of all active duty military personnel in GTMO.

UNIVERSITY OF FLORIDA

I ARRIVED IN Gainesville, Florida in September of 1961 with Jim Weeks. We had congregated in New Jersey and driven south to Gainesville with one of Jim's friends. Jim was my only acquaintance at the University of Florida at that time. As I mentioned earlier, I was transitioning from a graduating high school class of 8 to a freshman class of 2,400. I remember checking into my dorm at Graham Hall and noticing that in the distance from my room I could see some structures that included aqua blue plumbing pipes. I immediately sat down and wrote to my parents that Graham Hall was brand-new and air conditioned, and that it appeared that there was a swimming pool nearby. I later discovered that what I thought was a swimming pool was really a sewage treatment plant.

A counselor determined what classes I would take and fed a handful of data processing cards into a large computer. The computer made up my schedule, based on available classes. Since there were limited available classes that late into registration, the computer put together a horrendous class schedule that included some core classes, chemistry lab, writing lab, physical education, and ROTC. I was signed up for 16 credit hours that kept me in class for 25 hours a week. I had 7:30 a.m. classes with huge gaps between classes, except for Wednesdays when I had classes at all ends of the huge campus from 7:30 a.m. until 6:30 p.m. non-stop. I especially remember having a writing lab on Friday afternoons, starting at 5:30 p.m. Since the writing classroom was not air conditioned, the windows had to be opened, and we could hear the Kappa Alpha Fraternity partying across the street (since the weekend had begun for them). In subsequent semesters I learned the ropes of registering early and constructing a more effectively time-managed and efficient class schedule. I was in extreme culture shock. I was overwhelmed. I was homesick, but I was determined to make this college experience work. During freshman orientation I heard the proverbial message, "Look to your immediate left, look to your immediate right; two of you three will not make it to your sophomore year at the University of Florida." In spite of my being a valedictorian at tiny Sampson High School, I quickly discovered that I was competing with many people who were smarter than I was. I learned that in order to succeed at Florida, I was going to have to put more effort into preparing for tests and papers than many of my smarter fellow-students.

My physical education instructor mentioned to me one day that the freshman basketball coach, **Jim McCachren**, was searching for me and wanted me to report to him. Freshmen were not eligible to play inter-collegiate athletics in 1961, but they played a limited schedule with the intent of grooming athletes for the varsity team the next year. It seems that a letter had been forwarded from Norm Sloan, the University of Florida head basketball coach, to Coach McCachren about a star basketball player from William T. Sampson High School in Guantanamo Bay, Cuba, who should be considered to play basketball at Florida. The letter was written by a resident of Guantanamo Bay, and he really puffed me up as a phenomenal basketball prospect for the University of Florida. I eventually met with "Coach Mac," admitted to him that I didn't think that I was as good a basketball player as that letter portrayed, and respectfully declined the chance to try out for basketball.

I did want to give baseball at the University of Florida a try though. During the fall term I met with **Dave Fuller**, the Gator Baseball Coach. Since Coach Fuller had assistant football coach responsibilities, he wasn't too accessible for baseball activities until January. He did make arrangements for me to get a locker at the baseball stadium for informal workouts. During the informal workouts, I had the opportunity to meet some of the other freshmen baseball players, as well as some of the older varsity players. I learned that there was a talented freshman catcher from Leesburg, Florida named **Randy Burton**, who was on scholarship. As a "walk on," I had my work cut out for me, trying to make the freshman team as a catcher. I also learned that the freshman coach was a real entertaining guy named **P.A. Lee**. P.A. was maybe 5'6" tall and very skinny. A North Carolina native, he had a "folksy" personality and a gravelly voice and usually sported a large wad of chewing tobacco in his mouth. P.A. Lee and Dave Fuller would be my mentors for the next few years.

Reality confronted me as I returned from Christmas vacation. Final exams were scheduled for the third week in January, and I was going into finals with some shaky grades. Even though I brought all my textbooks with me to GTMO to study, I never opened a textbook during the vacation. Returning to Gainesville with my first "finals week" staring me in the face sure was depressing, but I studied hard and survived my first semester of college.

Freshman baseball tryouts were held at the beginning of the winter semester, and Coach P.A. Lee lived up to his billing as a funny, quirky character. I cherished my time on the baseball field. I experienced stress and uncertainty in the academic realm of my first year of college, but later in the afternoon when I dressed out and took the baseball field, I felt as if I was on vacation. I received another lift, when I learned that Randy Burton, the freshman catcher on scholarship, was out of the picture. Rumors circulated that Randy put too much effort into having a good time and not enough effort into his academics. He was one of those three students who were mentioned at freshman orientation. My window of opportunity to be a catcher at the University of Florida had opened slightly.

I made the freshman team, and started at catcher for most of the twenty-five games that we played that spring. We played other freshmen college teams and junior college teams. We even played at Raiford State Prison against the inmates, which was a unique experience. The prison baseball field was well maintained with concrete grandstands going down each foul line. At the time, the prison population was about 1,500. Racially, there were approximately 750 black prisoners and 750 white prisoners. Since there were not too many other forms of entertainment at Raiford, the games were well attended. The white prisoners all sat on the home team side, cheering for the inmates. The blacks all sat on the visitors' side, and we had a fan base of 750 black prisoners cheering for us. On one occasion, Coach Lee went out to discuss an umpire's call on a tag play at second base.

The crowd loved it. First he demonstrated the defensive player making a tag. Then he assumed the role of base runner, and demonstrated a hook slide. For effect, he demonstrated everything a second time. This skinny, short, bow-legged old man with a gravelly voice, and a wad of chewing tobacco in his mouth had 1,500 prison inmates rolling in the grandstands with uncontrolled laughter. In addition to being an educator and coach, P.A. Lee was a showman.

He enjoyed the game of baseball, and he made it fun for his players. Statistically, I enjoyed a good freshman year. I led the team in batting average, as a "slap hitter" without a lot of power. I got my share of lucky hits, and I seemed to have the knack of getting myself into trouble on the baseball field and then somehow escaping. Athletes often assume nicknames, and P.A. Lee was responsible for giving me the nickname of "Roses." We were playing St. Johns River Junior College in Palatka, and I had made a base running judgment error, getting caught in a rundown between second and third base. The rundown was misplayed, and I ended up being safe on third base. Two pitches later there was a wild pitch, and I scored the "go-ahead run," enabling us to win the game. After the game, P.A. reviewed with us what we had done wrong and what we had done well. Referring to my base running blunder, P.A. said, "And Kenworthy, you seem to have the ability to step in a pile of crap and come out smelling like a bouquet of roses." From that day on, my teammates and P.A. called me "Roses."

I thoroughly enjoyed every moment that I was on the baseball field at Florida. I was in my euphoric and happy zone. I am not sure if I would have ever attained a college degree, if it were not for playing baseball at the University of Florida. Playing freshman baseball set the stage for me to survive college.

Jim Weeks joined a social fraternity—Theta Chi. So naturally, I pledged Theta Chi, and Jim was my "big brother" in the spring of 1962. Initiation and hell week was not fun. There was hazing, and I received a few bruises; but, I made it and I became a "cool frat brother." There were advantages: a place to live and eat meals together, a place to party, the chance to socialize with some nice guys, and some other privileges. I was turned off by the phoniness of some of my brothers, but I felt that the social fraternity experience was helpful in many ways in my development as a young adult.

Three years later, I was asked by some brothers to run for president of Theta Chi. Apparently some of the brothers were not happy with a guy named **Bill Price**, who was aspiring to be president. In trying to find an opponent to run against Bill, my name surfaced. They felt I was a likeable guy, who might have a chance to defeat Bill. I perceived myself more likeable than qualified to be a fraternity president, but I agreed to run for president, if they couldn't find anybody better. I really didn't think that I had a chance to win the election. Three nights before the election my opponent did a faux pas. The code at the Theta Chi house was that girls were not allowed in the rooms upstairs. Brothers would sneak girls upstairs, but discretion was expected. Bill, his girlfriend, and another couple apparently blatantly went up to Bill's room and played strip poker. Even though our fraternity brothers were known to do some unethical, illegal, and illicit deeds, this indiscretion was considered a big scandal for someone wanting to be fraternity president. Bill lost several votes, and I won the election (by three votes). Otherwise, I never would have won without the scandal. Theta Chi was going through some austere times financially, and I did the best that I could. It was a good leadership experience, but I was relieved when my term expired.

The Cuban Missile Crisis occurred in the fall of 1962. The Soviet Union was installing missiles in Cuba, threatening our national security. I remember watching President Kennedy on television proclaiming that the U.S. was taking measures to confront the Soviets over this issue. He announced that all dependents were being evacuated from Guantanamo Bay immediately. World War III was imminent, and for three days I had no idea where my parents were. As a college student, I had a student deferment to prevent me from being drafted into the military; but, I was already making plans to enlist. This country 90 miles to our south was being utilized as a platform to be used to endanger us as a democratic nation. As history revealed, the Soviets backed down, removed its missile installations, and the crisis was quelled. I eventually learned that Lois was put on a ship for Norfolk, Virginia and stayed in Massachusetts for a few weeks. Ken stayed on the base, was issued a firearm (remember he was a planner and estimator for plumbing and electrical projects in GTMO), and was mandated to write a last will and testament by the Commanding Officer. Decades later, when

Ken passed away, I had a chance to read that will. It was crudely hand-written on a piece of lined notebook paper. While the major concern during the crisis was the looming Armageddon (World War III), I learned that Ken was also concerned that Lois, during her evacuation, would have free reign to their bank accounts in the United States (they had accounts in Norfolk, Fall River, and Miami, where Frank lived), and Lois was a more liberal spender than Ken.

Life as a student was literally and figuratively awesome with so many people and so much to do. As an example, one October night as a fresh-man, I went to study at the library, couldn't concentrate, and decided to quit early. On the way back to my dorm, I noticed a large cluster of students gathered around a lighted outdoor stage. The event was a skit competition for the upcoming homecoming event called "Gator Growl." The winners of the skit competition would have the opportunity to present their skits at "Gator Growl," which was held at Florida Field, the football stadium. The skits were creative, irreverent and hilarious; I was entertained for two hours. Jim had told me about "Gator Growl", which was held on Friday night of Homecoming Weekend before 50,000 students and alumni. It was a pep rally that included the aforementioned skits, a performance by the talented and rhythmic Florida A&M Band (a historically black university from Tallahassee), a famous music act, a nationally known comedian, and a huge fireworks display. Earlier in the day there was a parade.

Another example occurred in late February as I was going to an early morning class. I was walking by the Florida Gym (where the Gator basket-ball team played) and noticed dozens of school buses with hundreds of high school kids flowing into the gym. The Florida state high school basketball finals were being held in Gainesville. I decided to return to my dorm, drop off my textbooks, forget my schoolwork, and spend the next two days and nights watching numerous basketball games of high schools from all over the state of Florida.

Another example was the "Florida Relays" held in the spring. Collegiate and high school track and field athletes from all over the country converged at the University of Florida for one of the most prestigious track and field meets in the country at the time.

In addition to Homecoming Weekend, there were five or six other football weekends each fall. On Thursday nights before the Saturday games, alumni and other football fans would begin to converge in Gainesville, and excitement would mount. Florida Field held only about 53,000 fans (the capacity now approaches 90,000), but 53,000 was a huge crowd for a naïve small-timer from tiny Guantanamo Bay.

Esteemed artists and political science figures would regularly visit the U of F. I also loved going to Gator basketball games. I was caught up in the fraternity scene. I wanted to pursue intercollegiate baseball as far as I could take it. I was busy and awed by my college experience. After much consideration, I locked into a major in physical education with an emphasis on coaching athletics at a high school. Granted, it was a little easier course of study than some other considerations, but I made a decision to choose a field in which I could find comfort and enjoyment.

In the spring of 1963 I tried out for the varsity baseball team. Dave Fuller was the head baseball coach, and I was pretty intimidated by his toughness on the baseball field. He was a boxer in college, and stories vary that he either punched out or almost punched out an umpire at a game at Auburn University. I think he was aware that I led the freshman team in batting average, but he recognized that I had a swing that allowed me to make contact with the ball and minimized striking out. He realized that I lacked any hitting power. While P.A. Lee tagged me as "Roses," Dave Fuller gave me a new moniker—"Cunnythumper," a name he made up to describe my style of hitting. He also noted that while I had good reactions behind the plate as a catcher, I had a below average throwing arm. I made the team as a back-up catcher. One quality that I quickly perceived about Coach Fuller was his demeanor in his office, when I had occasion to visit him there. He was personable and helpful; on the field he was gruff and no-nonsense.

I even started the first three games of the season (in a very nervous state), because the starting catcher was recovering from an injury. After the starting catcher returned to play, I played occasionally during the remainder of the season. It was exciting to travel all over the south to other Southeastern Conference universities, playing in Athens, Georgia; Atlanta,

Georgia; Nashville, Tennessee; Knoxville, Tennessee; Lexington, Kentucky; and our nemesis in baseball in the early 60's: Auburn, Alabama. We mostly traveled by bus, which we called "The Blue Goose," but sometimes we would fly in an old DC 3 airplane, that was owned by the university. On more than one occasion I attempted to get right with my maker, before boarding that plane. Most of my teammates had similar trepidations about that airplane.

On the last road trip of my sophomore season, Coach Fuller called me up to the front of the bus to inform me that he was putting me on scholarship for the next year. It wasn't a full scholarship, but it would cover two-thirds of my college expenses. I couldn't wait to write to Ken and Lois (especially Ken, since he was the one hoping and praying that I wouldn't get accepted to the more expensive Dartmouth College two years before). Upon graduating from high school, I had received some scholarship money for my academics that helped take some of the strain of funding my college education off my parents. My status up until this time was a "walk on." While the baseball scholarship helped my parents financially, elevating my status from "walk on" to the holder of an athletic scholarship gave me a great feeling of accomplishment also.

In the spring of 1964 I suffered a shoulder separation during pre-season practice, and I abruptly became a medical redshirt for that year. I never played an inning that year. I spent the whole season traveling with the team, serving as batting practice catcher and bullpen catcher—frustrating, but better than doing nothing.

The next two years I was a starting catcher—sort of. Coach Fuller platooned me with another catcher; which meant that I (being a left-handed hitter) started against right-handed pitchers and a right-handed hitting catcher started against opposing left-handed pitchers.

I received my Bachelor's Degree in Physical Education and Health in May of 1965. I subsequently learned that I could use my last year of baseball eligibility while pursuing my master's degree in physical education. That last year I was elected captain by my teammates and played well enough to make the All-SEC 2nd team as a catcher.

GATOR CATCHER JACK KENWORTHY
... he's set for Georgia series

**My years as a Gator baseballer were filled with many
rewarding experiences. I am not sure if I would have ever
successfully acquired any college degrees without my
"baseball fix" to accompany my college studies.**

I felt that Coach Fuller gained more confidence in me during my junior and senior years of eligibility—even more confidence than I had in myself with my limited hitting and throwing skills. I considered myself an over-
achieving college baseball player, who would really like a shot in professional baseball; but, it was not meant to be. Coach Fuller was instrumental
in my acquiring my first job—Assistant Baseball Coach at Brevard Junior
College. In the spring of 1966 Brevard Junior College was playing the
Florida Freshman team, still under the helm of P.A. Lee. The coach of BJC,
Bob Aitken, mentioned to P.A. that he was looking for an assistant coach

with a master's degree in physical education to teach physical education activity classes at the college (many colleges and junior colleges had a physical education requirement for all students then). While I was very young and lacked any experience in coaching and teaching, I met the criteria. Dave Fuller and P.A. Lee collectively recommended me for the job, and I was selected.

As years went by, another Gator baseball player, **Jerry Nicolson**, taught and coached tennis at Brevard Community College. Jerry was a standout pitcher at U of F when I was a freshman there. I remember Jerry took time to offer words of encouragement to me, an overwhelmed and insecure freshman baseball player. Jerry and I have maintained a friendship since 1962. Starting in the 1990's we decided that we should try to plan trips to Gainesville to visit Dave Fuller, who was then retired and still living there. We both felt that Dave had enormous influence in helping to shape both of our lives, and we wanted to pay tribute to him. We took annual trips to visit Dave. A few years ago there was a best-selling book, entitled Tuesdays with Morrie by Mitch Albom. The author of the book would visit his former esteemed professor every Tuesday to discuss intellectual and academic topics. I likened our visits with our old coach to visits Mitch Albom cites in his book—the difference being that we were "ex-jocks," and the conversations were usually not too intellectual or academic.

Dave passed away a few years ago, and his family asked me to say a few words at his memorial service. I was honored to have been asked. I shared the podium with some of the legends of University of Florida athletics. In my remarks, I mentioned that when I became a coach, I felt that now I had earned the right to call him "Dave." After a couple of years, I realized that I felt uncomfortable calling him "Dave." The moniker "Coach" was more appropriate. Good coaches display concern and care for their players and students. Good coaches stress the importance of hard work, teamwork, cooperation, competitiveness, setting goals, and responding to adversity and challenges—all lessons that can be applied to living life. They also admonish their charges, when it is appropriate. Out of respect I will always refer to "Dave" as "Coach." Likewise, P.A. Lee and Les West will always be "Coach." Occasionally I am still referred to as "Coach," and I accept that title with honor and pride (even though they may be calling me coach, because they remember that I was a coach but can't remember my name).

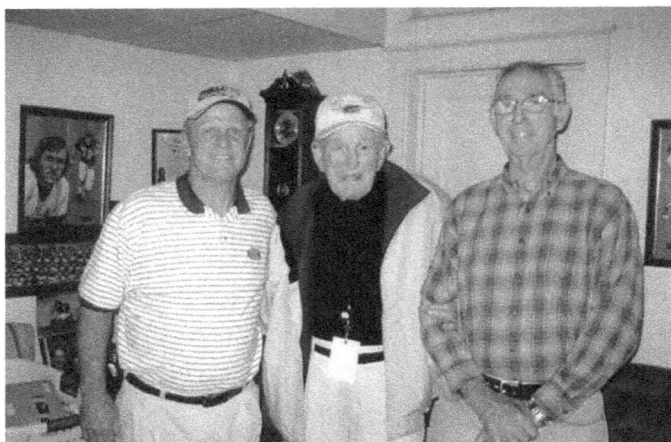

Jerry Nicolson (on right) and I flank Coach Dave Fuller circa 2007. Jerry and I both felt that "Coach" was very influential to us. We visited him in Gainesville for many years to pay our respects.

During my graduate school year of 1965-66, I picked up still another nickname. My Gator teammates gave me this new name when I was elected to be a University of Florida Honor Court Justice. Some student government politicos suggested that I get on the ballot as a justice, representing the political party of the Theta Chi fraternity. If a student was caught cheating, he could take his/her case to the Honor Court, where law students could practice prosecuting and defending, and Honor Court Justices would serve on the jury. My new nickname was "Judge." So, many people who knew Jack at the University of Florida referred to Jack as either "Roses," "Cunnythumper," or "Judge." **Kip Marchman** was one of my roommates in Gainesville who became an attorney in Winter Park, Florida. I still stay in touch with Kip occasionally. When I call his law office, I tell his receptionist that I am "Judge Kenworthy;" she gets him on the phone promptly.

In early August 1966 I had completed all of my coursework for my Master's Degree with only my "oral examination" lurking before me. The "orals" consisted of me being in a room with three professors, as they grilled me with questions, based on a twenty-page paper that I had prepared for them. The paper consisted of the philosophies of learning, the values of health and physical education in our society, and my assessment of how well the College of Health, Physical Education, and Recreation at the University of Florida had prepared me for my new profession. I was torn between telling the committee what they wanted to hear and giving them my heartfelt opinions. Surely, the committee would be interested in some of my criticism with my five years of experience as a college student. I criticized, and that was a mistake. I could sense that the committee was really irritated with what I had to say. Additionally, I had misspelled the name of one of the committee members on the paper that I had prepared. The scheduled two-hour session was extended an extra hour, and at one time I was asked to leave the room for fifteen minutes, so they could discuss me. After three grueling hours, I was told that I had passed—barely. I took my Master's Degree and ran.

JACKGLO

This photo was taken June 4, 1966 at Grace Episcopal Church in Ocala, Florida. Horned-rim glasses were stylish at that time.

I MET MY future wife and lifetime partner, **Gloria Fugate**, on a blind date in the summer of 1965. Kip (mentioned above) and his future wife, **Donna**, introduced us.

Gloria and I use the moniker, JACKGLO, as a user ID to navigate our way through our computer for our family matters online, so JACKGLO is an appropriate term to name our approximately half a century relationship.

The summer before graduate school I had to stay in Gainesville. Someone got me a job, working on the loading platform of a chicken processing plant. Live chickens would arrive by truck early in the morning, and by the end of the day they would leave the plant in wooden crates dead and packed in ice onto tractor trailers that would supply chicken to grocery stores throughout the state of Florida. A normal work day entailed: arriving at the plant around 6 a.m., working until 10 a.m., taking time off work for the next four hours, then returning to work around 2 p.m. for another four hours of loading trucks. All of this physical work occurred during the extreme summer heat. While minimum wage at that time was $1.25 per hour, the plant manager paid me $1.35 per hour. I received this boost in pay, if I would travel through a really poor and seedy section of town to wake up several of his other employees at 5:30 a.m. My efforts ensured that they would show up for work. Two-thirds of my fellow employees had spent some time in county jails or at Raiford State Prison. In other words, this was one crappy job, but I was hoping to lift up my quality of life with a date with a girl.

My roommate, Kip, mentioned that his girlfriend, Donna, had a roommate named Gloria who might be interested in a blind date. It was hinted that Gloria had a tendency to be outspoken and opinionated. Almost fifty years of history has proven that assessment to be accurate; so, I guess I knew what I was getting into. Two hours into our double-date, Gloria got irritated with some insignificant thing that Kip had said and let him know about it. You could say that I experienced some "coming attractions" to what my future held. In spite of her feisty ways, Gloria has proven to be a loyal and loving wife, mother, and grandmother.

Gloria was born and raised in Ocala, the youngest daughter of a cattle rancher and watermelon farmer. She was a fourth generation Floridian, whose ancestors came to Florida in the 1840's before Florida was declared a state. Her family could be described as "Florida Crackers." Like me, she was the youngest sibling in her family by several years. She was majoring in Elementary Education at Florida. We seemed to hit it off well, and within months we were engaged.

I had girlfriends in high school. **Betty Sanderson** was a somewhat serious girlfriend; but, when I went to Gainesville it became mostly a long-distance relationship. She went to school in GTMO and subsequently moved to Tennessee. She came to Gainesville for Homecoming of 1961, and that was romantic. We wrote each other faithfully (remember, we had no texting or email), and I would call when I could get enough coins together (remember, we didn't have cell phones with anytime free minutes). As months progressed, our letters and phone calls became less frequent until one month I called, and Betty's mother answered and awkwardly informed me that Betty had married someone in Tennessee. Ironically, I ran into Betty in Nashville, Tennessee during my sophomore season of baseball. The Gators were playing Vanderbilt, and the team was eating at a Morrison's Cafeteria in downtown Nashville. Four places behind me in line stood Betty in a pregnant state. We had a stilted twenty-minute conversation about old times.

Another girlfriend was arranged by (of all people) my mother, Lois. As I was returning from college to GTMO for a visit, Lois set me up with a date with **Gerry Swanson**, a Navy chaplain's daughter. Lois liked the idea of me being influenced indirectly by a "man of the cloth." Lois really did me well. Gerry was pretty with a good personality and nice looking legs. Way to go, Lois! I had a renewed appreciation for my mother. Gerry was going to college in Virginia, and her chaplain father was being transferred to North Carolina. The result was another long-distance relationship destined to fail. We had limited face-to-face time together, and our letters became further and further apart. I finally got the message. I think Gerry dumped me. I had plenty of dates at college, but Betty and Gerry have always stood out as the two most prominent. Then Gloria came entered my life.

Gloria and I set a wedding date for June 4, 1966. Because Gloria was not affiliated with any particular church denomination, we decided to get married in an Episcopal Church in Ocala. Gloria's parents (**Murray and Martha Fugate**) informed us that the wedding was going to be small, since

Gloria's older sister, Bette, had a simple and inexpensive wedding many years before. The early June date was not convenient for Gloria's father, Murray; because, that was in the middle of his watermelon picking season, and trucks were lined up at his packing shed to transport his watermelons all over the country. He reluctantly sacrificed two hours of his busy day to marry off his daughter and then returned to the packing shed. I am not sure how thrilled Murray was, marrying off his daughter to a "Yankee."

I remember the vows that I took on that day, and I fully intended to honor those vows then, as I do now. I faintly recall items such as loving her, comforting her, and keeping her in sickness and health, as long as we both shall live. Other declarations that were mentioned in that ceremony were for better or worse, richer or poorer till death do us part. Those were some scary and demanding vows for a 23-year old guy to take, when his major focus at the time was some lovemaking later in the evening. Gloria and Jack became a wedded couple on that day, and we have been a team for almost 50 years.

The small and simple reception consisted of sandwiches, cake, and punch. We escaped to St. Augustine for a two-night honeymoon. At first, it appeared that we would only have enough money for a one-night honeymoon, but some people gave us some cash at the reception, allowing us to extend the honeymoon. I can't prove it, but I suspect that the motel clerk at the St. Augustine motel was playing games with us on our honeymoon night. It was probably apparent that we had just married. I was not able to unlock the door to the motel room. I returned to the front desk to report the problem. He handed me another key and said, "Oh, I must have given you the wrong key." I detected that the clerk was trying to subdue a smile on his face.

We returned to Gainesville to our first apartment in a bad section of town. The rent was $60 a month. Earlier we had seen an apartment for $50 a month, but it had no door to the bathroom—only a curtain. We decided that the bathroom door was worth the additional $10. The duration of the summer of 1966 was devoted to the completion of our college work and securing employment.

Coach Lee and Coach Fuller had arranged for me to have an interview with Bob Aitken, the Head Baseball Coach and Physical Education

Department Chairman at Brevard Junior College in Cocoa, Florida. The Cocoa area was booming with an influx of people attracted to the employment opportunities of the nascent space program at the Kennedy Space Center. Bob's wife, Carolyn, was an elementary school teacher in the area, and she arranged for Gloria to interview for a teaching job. The trip was productive. Gloria secured an elementary school teaching job in nearby Merritt Island. I was offered a position as Physical Education Instructor and Assistant Baseball Coach at Brevard Junior College.

Gloria and I came from two different cultures:

- Jack was an uprooted lower middle-class Yankee who transitioned into the lifestyle of a military brat on a naval base.
- Gloria was a daughter of a cattle rancher and watermelon farmer; she would qualify as a "Florida Cracker," who had hardly ever been out of Marion County, Florida in her life until our marriage.

My only mentors for making a marriage work were Ken and Lois (and perhaps Ozzie and Harriet from the television show). Gloria's mentors were Murray and Martha. We merged together from two entirely different cultures.

We rented a modern apartment on the Indian River in Merritt Island. Gloria's school was nearby; she could get there and back by taking all right turns. We chose St. Luke's Episcopal Church out in the country in North Merritt Island for our church. Gloria made plans to become an Episcopalian and began taking confirmation classes, but it was determined that Gloria had not been baptized. The priest, **Father Paul Perrine**, became a friend. He was outspoken and had the ability to irritate his congregation members by freely giving his opinion about anything. This meant that he could get under the skin of the irascible Gloria. At one gathering he jokingly referred to the un-baptized Gloria as a "heathen." I have already hinted that Gloria was easy to irritate, and the "heathen" reference set her off. She threatened to remain a heathen, but she was ultimately baptized and confirmed to become an Episcopalian. She forgave and recovered, and to this day loves being an Episcopalian.

Gloria and I spent our first Christmas together in Guantanamo Bay. Ken and Lois were still there, and it was arranged for us to catch a navy seaplane from Jamaica to GTMO. We flew commercially from Miami to Kingston, Jamaica and then connected with a seaplane to GTMO. Gloria had an opportunity to see my hometown of six years. A week later Ken and Lois accompanied us on the seaplane to Kingston with the idea that we could spend four more hours together before they took the seaplane back to GTMO. Our flight to Miami was scheduled a couple of hours after they left. It was New Years Eve, and the seaplane crew of four took some "leisure time" in Kingston during their four-hour layover. We saw them return to the seaplane, and three of them appeared pretty drunk. I remember hoping and praying that the one that appeared sober was the pilot. Regardless, they made it safely back to GTMO.

Even though we are opposites in many areas, Gloria and I continue to make this relationship work almost 50 years later. Our relationship is based on respect for each other and each other's ideals. Monogamous relationships are not easy; the 50% divorce rate attests to that. God obviously designed males and females to be attractive to each other, in order to facilitate the procreation of the species. Like most guys, I find the female of our species to be attractive. Through respect for Gloria and with a ton of will power, JACKGLO will prevail and are in this for the long haul.

I went into this relationship with Gloria with a hint of what she was like, remembering how easily Kip got under her skin on our initial double date. I bought into her tendency toward being easily angered, overdramatic, with a sprinkling of hypochondria as part of the total package. Like most females (so I am told), her moods shift from day to day and throughout the day. I was aware of all of these aspects of Gloria, while I was at the altar of Grace Episcopal Church on June 4, 1966. Also I am sure that Gloria can elaborate on how difficult I am to live with. In summary, we are pretty much direct opposites. Gloria probably is irritated that I don't worry enough, but I try to find a positive out of any negative situation. I have sometimes been accused of looking at life too often through "rose-colored glasses." She fails to understand how I often turn to humor (sometimes corny humor) to help me through tough times that I cannot control.

Some chapters in Jack and Gloria's marriage include:

- Learning to adapt to each other (we're still learning).
- Being neophyte parents of infants, children, and teenagers.
- Jack, trying to establish himself as a respected baseball coach and a health/physical education instructor.
- Gloria, learning to be a mother. She was a good one. She took an 18-year hiatus from full-time employment to be a totally involved mother.
- Jack, trying to juggle being a husband, father, baseball coach, and health/physical education assistant professor (and falling short in all of those roles).
- Jack, wishing he could be like his bachelor friend, **Chuck Underhill**, three out of seven days a week, because Chuck would go home to a quiet home and do whatever he wanted; Jack would go home to a variety of family mini-crises. The other four days of the week, Jack liked the idea of our family dynamics.
- Jack and Gloria, having to do some adjusting of principles, as our kids became teenagers. (I think having teenagers strengthened our marriage; those years were so scary that we felt it was us against them, causing Gloria and me to close ranks as parents).
- Jack and Gloria in later years, trying to adjust to being "empty nesters," as our children went out into the world in later years.

JACKGLO in later years.

BREVARD COMMUNITY COLLEGE

IN AUGUST 1966 Gloria and I drove to our new apartment in Merritt Island. She was in her 1962 Mercury and I was in my 1953 Studebaker. We were able to pack all of our earthly possessions in those two vehicles with room to spare. In spite of the objection of Gloria's parents, Murray and Martha, we were beginning our life together away from Ocala.

During the mid-sixties the Florida Junior College System was forming. The premise of the junior college system was to locate junior colleges (later re-named community colleges) throughout the state. The goal was to provide the citizens of Florida with the opportunity to complete their first two years of a college education and/or training in technical or vocational areas to prepare them for enhanced employment opportunities. The sites of these junior colleges were determined by population density, attempting to enable citizens to live within 45 minutes of a campus. Additionally, tuition prices would be more affordable than those at a four-year university. Entrance requirements at junior colleges were pretty liberal; all you basically needed for admission were a high school diploma and a heartbeat.

The junior college concept was a positive movement for all of Florida. It provided advancement possibilities for almost everyone, and it represented "hope" for almost everyone. The typical junior college student body consisted of those who could not afford to go away to a college, those who did not perform well in high school, the working population taking courses part-time to improve themselves, people wanting to attain marketable skills, wives and female divorcees seeking skills to get into the workforce for the first time, young adults who did not particularly know what they wanted to do, those who flunked out of another college, or those who ran out of money while attending an out-of-town college. The student population at Brevard Junior College encompassed an eclectic and representative sampling of the citizens of Brevard County—from rich to poor, from intelligent to dull. In my thirty years at Brevard Junior (Community) College, I embraced the community college concept. When I first arrived at Brevard, the institution was called "Brevard Junior College;" a few years later it was renamed "Brevard Community College;" in 2013 it was renamed "Eastern Florida State College." In this book I will refer to this institution as "Brevard Community College." While some enjoy belittling community colleges in comparison with "more esteemed" four-year colleges and universities, I believe that they represent hope to almost everyone. Ultimately twenty-eight community colleges evolved throughout Florida with most colleges having multiple campuses. BCC eventually had four campuses.

At the inception of the community college system, the Florida state legislature mandated that these junior colleges would not have football programs for fear that expenditures would be excessive and get out of control. But, basketball and baseball evolved at almost all of these community colleges. Florida's baseball-friendly climate contributed to a rapid growth in baseball programs throughout the state. Many high school baseball players from states to the north were encouraged to enroll in Florida community colleges, where they could get more baseball playing time and exposure. Major league baseball scouts and four-year college coaches were encouraging aspiring baseball players to go to Florida community colleges, because they recognized the high quality of baseball skill being played.

In the sixties, most colleges and community colleges offered physical education activity classes as a requirement for being awarded a college degree. Brevard Community College required four college credit hours of physical education in order for a student to receive a two-year degree. The college required that faculty have a master's degree in that subject area, in order to teach. My Masters of Physical Education and Health qualified me to teach these activity courses, and my experience as a college baseball player gave me some credentials to acquire my first job, even though I was extremely young and inexperienced.

**Jack and Bob Aitken. Bob was responsible for hiring me at
Brevard Junior College, later to be named
Brevard Community College.**

Conveniently, Bob Aitken was the Head Baseball Coach and the Chairman of the Physical Education Department. He was ultimately responsible for my first job, for which I am eternally grateful. Bob intimated to me that he planned to step down as baseball coach in the next couple of years, and I could possibly step into the head coaching job at that time. Bob was supportive throughout my 30 years at Brevard, and I considered him my friend. Bob advanced to become a Campus Provost and College Vice-President at Brevard Community College. I felt that while he always treated me fairly and with respect, he could get real nasty with many of his subordinates. Decades later I went to his retirement reception at the college. I informed him that the reception was very well attended, because most people were there to make sure that he hadn't changed his mind about retiring.

My work at BCC kept me really busy. In the morning hours I was teaching physical education classes with an average of 35 students per class. I was teaching physical fitness, tennis, weight training, team sports, bowling, and other activity classes. I was a rookie, novice instructor only a few years older than my students. It took a lot of planning and preparation, trying to keep 35 students functionally busy while learning some of the skills myself. I also was in charge of an intramural sports program. In the afternoon, my responsibilities shifted to the baseball program. Bob Aitken had recruited players from all over the country. We made arrangements for apartments for the players, registering them for classes, picking them up at the Orlando airport, performing administrative tasks for those on scholarship, developing the spring schedule, ordering equipment, monitoring student-athlete progress (trying to keep them academically eligible), and many other duties (I almost forgot—coaching baseball and conducting practice and games). If it had anything to do with baseball, Bob and I did it all. **Jim Oler** was the Athletic Director, but he was also the Head Basketball Coach, and most of his efforts went to his own program. We were a severely under-staffed athletic department, trying to produce a quality athletic program. Amid all of the hard work, confusion and complexity, we did a pretty good job. In the spring, our playing schedule kept us travelling all over the state of Florida in station wagons or vans, and the coaches did the driving.

The quality of baseball in Florida's community colleges was phenomenal. Florida community college baseball players were regularly advancing into professional baseball or transferring to reputable NCAA baseball programs. Two very successful major league pitchers who started out as Florida community college baseball players in the 1960's were Don Sutton (from Gulf Coast Community College) and Steve Carlton (from Miami-Dade Community College). Both were subsequently inducted into Major League Baseball's Hall of Fame. Over one hundred former Florida community college baseball players have worn major league uniforms in the last five decades.

Brevard had two future major leaguers on its 1968 roster, when I was still an assistant coach. **Bill Stein** was an infielder for over 10 years with the St. Louis Cardinals, Seattle Mariners, and the Texas Rangers. He still holds an American League pinch hitting record. **Tom Walker** was a right-handed pitcher with the Montreal Expos and the Detroit Tigers (and other teams). Gloria and I visited Bill and Tom on a few occasions during their major league careers. They would leave complimentary tickets for their former assistant coach. I especially remember the Tigers coming to play the Boston Red Sox at Fenway Park in 1975. Tom was a bullpen pitcher with the Tigers. Gloria and I went to a Friday and a Saturday game. After the Friday night game, we went out to eat with Tom. I mentioned to Tom that my mother, Lois, had been diagnosed with cancer and her prognosis was not good. I went on to mention that Red Sox outfielder Carl Yastrzemski was her favorite baseball player, and that my father, Ken, thought that "Yaz" was a bum. Tom said he was pretty good friends with Carl, and he volunteered to get an autographed baseball for Lois. The next day at the ballpark, Tom got my attention before the game and threw me a baseball with the inscription "Regards to Lois, Carl Yastrzemski." I was thrilled to give the baseball to Lois in her weakened state; I think she was excited about it. I later learned that Tom was friends with the late Roberto Clemente, a Pittsburgh Pirate Hall of Famer who died in a plane crash in 1972. Clemente was delivering supplies to Nicaragua, which was recovering from a devastating earthquake. Tom offered to go on that plane with Roberto; Roberto said thanks, but the plane was too full for any more people. So, Tom is still around and living in Pittsburgh, watching his son, Neil, play second base for the Pittsburgh Pirates.

No children were in the picture for our first two and a half years of marriage. We traveled a little and started buying a few things like furniture and newer cars. While I was busy learning how to be a physical education instructor and an assistant baseball coach, I was still an "assistant." This meant that I wasn't assuming the full accountability of being a head coach. In the summer of 1968, all that would change. We learned that Gloria was pregnant and that Bob Aitken was stepping down as head baseball coach, and I was appointed the new head coach. I thought life had been busy; it was really going to get busy now, and it wasn't going to slow down for a few decades.

JACK AS HEAD BASEBALL COACH AT BREVARD COMMUNITY COLLEGE

This picture shows me operating in the third base coaching box. Over twelve years, I spent thousands of hours in the third base coaching box.

BEING THE HEAD baseball coach was much more different than being an assistant coach. As an assistant, I was a confidant to the players, a sounding board, a liaison between the players and the head coach. I had my limited scope of responsibility as an assistant, but when I was promoted to head baseball coach, I became the "decision-maker." While Bob Aitken had an assistant coach (me), I had no assistant, when I was promoted to head coach. The job description was extremely demanding, but I was young and ambitious and determined to keep BCC baseball competitive at the state level.

Some of the duties of head baseball coach (without any real assistance) included:

- Continuously recruiting high school baseball talent
- Managing equipment
- Formulating and facilitating a budget
- Arranging for team transportation (which included being a van driver)
- Overseeing academic registration for my baseball athletes
- Planning meals and lodging for away games
- Baseball field maintenance (a year around task)
- Being a disciplinarian
- Being a team chaplain
- Raising funds
- Formulating fall and spring baseball schedules
- Gathering athlete eligibility documents
- Promoting the BCC baseball program by giving speeches and making appearances
- Teaching and coaching baseball skills and strategies on the field

In addition to all of the responsibilities listed above, I was expected to teach six or seven sections of health, fitness, and sports classes each term—

about 20 hours per week. Being a coach is a very demanding profession. You are constantly competing; a won-loss record is traditionally placed after your name in parentheses. Your day's tasks are never really complete. If you decide to take some time off from recruiting potential high school baseball athletes, you can be assured that two or three other competing college coaches will be actively recruiting them. On several occasions, I had received phone calls in the middle of the night to be informed that an athlete was involved in an automobile accident, was in trouble with the law, was being disruptive, or was violating some rules at an apartment complex. One night I received a phone call from an irate father who informed me that one of my ballplayers had impregnated his daughter. He informed me that she needed an abortion and expected my ballplayer to fund the abortion. He asked me what I was going to do about it. I guess the father expected that one of my duties was facilitating the funding of abortions. For the record, I confronted the player about the phone call. He said that the father of that baby could be any of ten other guys. I never followed-up on the outcome of that issue. I didn't consider funding abortions as one of the job descriptions as baseball coach.

Being a mentor and disciplinarian overseeing twenty 19-year old guys was a demanding challenge, especially for a coach who was just a few years older than his athletes (in the earlier coaching years). I tried to be a player-friendly coach with finite expectations of my players. Team rules were defined, and I attempted to be consistent in the enforcement of the rules. Realizing that 19-year old college athletes can do some irresponsible and knucklehead deeds, I tried to follow the principle that my players were entitled to a second chance; but, don't expect a third chance.

As a coach, I tried to help my athletes. One ballplayer I remember in my early coaching years was **Joe Miedreich**, a catcher from one of the boroughs of New York City. One of the team rules was that you didn't just miss practice; you were required to contact me in advance to give me a reason why you had to miss practice. Joe called me one morning to tell me that he had a toothache and was going to the dentist and could not make practice. That was fine with me. Toothaches happen. On the next day, Joe came to the office and told me that he had been to the dentist. I asked him which dentist he saw. Joe said he didn't remember the dentist's name. I mentioned that I knew a couple of local dentists, and if he was treated by a dentist that I knew, perhaps I could call and maybe get him a discount on his bill. I proceeded to open the phone book yellow pages and found the 15 or 20 local dentists listed in the book, and asked him if any of the names looked familiar. I sincerely wanted to help reduce his dental bill, if I could. As luck (Joe's bad luck) would have it, Joe pointed out the name "Dr. Sharp" among the names listed in the yellow pages. To Joe's misfortune, Dr. Sharp happened to be my dentist. I immediately started to dial Dr. Sharp's office, telling Joe that I bet that I can get your bill reduced. Joe interrupted me and insisted that I put the phone down. He admitted that it was all a lie; he didn't have a toothache, and he didn't have a good excuse for missing practice. He paid the price for the lie, but he got a second chance.

On another occasion, a player informed me that he had to go to his grandfather's funeral in Kentucky and would have to miss three days of practice. Permission was granted. Three weeks later, I happened to run into the player's father at a local retail store. I inquired if it was his father or his wife's father who passed away in Kentucky. I was going to offer my condolences, but I was told that no grandfather had a funeral recently. The player was busted and paid the price for the lie. Once again, I meant well and caught someone in a lie.

Not everyone lied. A pitcher named **Bob Hudson** missed four days of fall practice in a row. When he finally returned, I asked him where he had been. He said, "Coach, you wouldn't understand. I was in Cape Hatteras, North Carolina in search of the perfect wave." Bob was an avid surfer, and apparently there was tropical storm activity off the Cape Hatteras coast. He paid the price and got a second chance. But, he was honest and up front with me.

John Fischetti was a big, strapping right-handed pitcher with some potential from near New York City. Bob Aitken had recruited him the year before, and he had some success as a freshman. As a sophomore, he was slated to be one of my starting pitchers in my first year as head coach. In the fall of my first year at the helm, John had committed some indiscretion (I can't remember what he did). I called him into my office and gave him a temporary suspension with a warning that he was being placed on a short leash. About a month later I received word that there was extensive dry wall damage in his apartment. I discovered that John had taken a baseball bat to three of the walls in his apartment with a little help from some alcohol. That was it. He had already had his second chance. I permanently suspended him from the team. This was my first test as a head coach, and I was comfortable that I had made a fair decision to kick him off the team. I received several long-distance phone calls from John's father the next few nights. He kept repeating in his Italian-American dialect, "Coach, my boy is a good boy. Give him another chance." I stuck to my guns and did not allow John back on the team. The movie "The Godfather" was released the next year. The movie portrayed how ruthless, vindictive, and violent certain Italian-Americans could be, if they were crossed. Some of the characters in that movie made me think of Mr. Fischetti. I often wonder if that movie had been released a year earlier, I may have succumbed, and John may have been given a third chance to play for me. I must stress that Mr. Fischetti was respectful on the phone and never threatened me in any way—he just sounded like some of those characters in "The Godfather." I had the opportunity to reunite with John several years later. We had a cordial conversation about his playing days and caught up with each other's lives. He asserted that he deserved his suspension and held no ill will toward me.

I had another New Yorker on the pitching staff in my first year of being the head coach. Since my predecessor, Bob Aitken, had recruited in the New York City area, I realized an influx of somewhat talented 19 year-old baseball players from NYC into Brevard County. **John Ceprini** was a pretty effective sophomore pitcher for the 1969 BCC Baseball Titans. John was drafted in the major league June draft by the Detroit Tigers and had a brief minor league career in the Appalachian League. I had heard a rumor that John went into law enforcement in Long Island after he finished his baseball career.

Several years passed. One day in the late 1970's, a long-haired somewhat disheveled-looking young adult came to my Melbourne Campus office and asked if I was Coach Kenworthy. When I said that I was, he said that he had come to say thank you. It seems that he was in Long Island over the summer, driving around in a "hippy van" (his description). He said that he had some illegal marijuana in that van, when he was pulled over by a policeman. As he was attempting to get his driver's license out of his wallet, his Brevard Community College library card fell out onto the ground. The policeman picked it up, and asked him if he went to Brevard Community College in Florida. Then the policeman asked if he knew Coach Kenworthy. The young man told me that day, "I didn't know you, Coach, but I said that I did." The policeman went on to tell the young man that he had played baseball at BCC for two years, and that he had many fond memories of Brevard County. He proceeded to gave him back his license without searching his van, and told him to have a nice evening. I suspect that policeman had to be John Ceprini. A couple of years ago I reunited with John. He is now retired from law enforcement and is a baseball scout for the Tampa Bay Rays. When I related that story, he smiled but did not acknowledge that it happened (probably the wisest thing for an ex-cop to do).

Speaking of long hair, one day I went to my barber, Gino, to get my regular haircut. As I got out of the barber chair, I reached for my wallet. "No charge today, Coach" he said. It seems that in the early to mid 70's, longer hair and facial hair was gaining popularity among college students. I tried to bend with the times and liberalized my hair policy, but within limits. During one particular team meeting, I informed ten of the team members that their hair was too straggly and needed a trim—and the deadline to do this was the next day (a week before my free haircut), or else they could not practice. The rule was if players could not practice, they could not play. As we started practice the next day, I noted that six of those ten guys still had hair that was too long. I told them that they could not practice, and if they still wanted to play at Brevard, they needed haircuts. In passing, I happened to mention that "Gino's Barbershop" was 3 miles away. They left and returned all properly trimmed within an hour. Gino enjoyed a windfall profit that afternoon and showed his appreciation by giving me a complimentary haircut.

I coached baseball for a total of 14 years. We would start each fall with between 40 and 80 potential ballplayers. We had dozens of dropouts each academic year for various reasons—bad grades, knucklehead behavior, injuries, family issues, money issues, paternity, and countless other reasons. We did offer partial scholarships, so I recruited, meeting lots of people who never came to BCC. I generally pared down to a roster of 19 players in the spring. The point is that there is a huge database of "people who knew Jack" through my baseball coaching endeavors—thousands of people.

I could write stories of at least a hundred former players who stood out in my memories. **Mike Lawson** from Melbourne High School was one of them. Mike, the first pitcher that I recruited, is one I remember. If a pitcher has command of the strike zone, can change speeds, and has movement on his pitches, he can keep you competitive in most games. He can also make his coach look better than he really is. Mike was that type of college pitcher. I had a reunion with Mike last year. Prior to that reunion, I had last seen Mike in Orlando in May of 1970. We had just been eliminated from the Florida Community College State Tournament, and we were having a catered post-game meal as a team. Mike was somewhat of a rogue. As we were finishing the meal, Mike decided to push the envelope and light up a cigarette. The whole team turned to see how I would react to this. Mike was a sophomore, and I no longer had authority over his behavior as a team member. I quickly tried to manufacture in my mind some acceptable response. I told Mike in front of the team that he could smoke, if he wanted to; but, he would have to pay for his own meal (BCC paid for the pre-game and post-game meals). He quickly snuffed out the cigarette, everyone laughed, and I picked up the tab.

Another pitcher who almost always kept us close in games was **Chuck Dale** from Gainesville, Florida. His coach told me that he does not look overly impressive pitching in the bullpen; but, when the game is on the line, there is no one else that you want on the mound. His coach, **Bob Hawkins** (a former teammate of mine at UF), described him perfectly. Any coach will tell you that there are certain players who cave in under pressure and others you can count on when the game is on the line. The coaching trick is to have the ability to identify and discern your talent. You could say that Chuck had the guts of a burglar, when he was on the mound. After two years at BCC, he went on to pitch at the University of Florida. He was drafted by the Boston Red Sox and pitched in their minor league system for a few years. Chuck was a bulldog of a competitor on the field, but in his mind once the game was over, he reverted to an easy-going demeanor, as if it were just a game (which it was). I had my share of baseball athletes who were the antithesis of Chuck—intense before and after the game and not too productive in the heat of action.

I received disturbing news several years ago. Chuck was noticing that he was losing distance on his drives on the golf course. He especially was concerned when his wife, **Jean**, consistently was out-driving him. After several tests, Chuck was diagnosed with amyotrophic lateral sclerosis or ALS, Lou Gehrig's Disease. I had occasion to spend a little time with Chuck during the year and a half from his diagnosis to his death. What a cruel disease! His mind stayed sharp, while his movement, physiological function, and speech continually deteriorated. I admired Chuck's courage. **Mike Worner**, a former teammate of Chuck's, and I went to a University of Central Florida baseball game to see **Jay Bergman**, who coached at UCF. Jay was Chuck's coach at the University of Florida. When Jay asked Chuck how he was doing, Chuck had a great answer. He said that the future did not look promising, but that he was going to battle ALS, as if he was on the mound with the bases loaded and nobody out. He would fight it with all he had. His mind was sharp right up until the end, but his mind was a prisoner in his own body. Sometimes I think that it would have been more humane if his mind would have deteriorated along with his other nerve function. Chuck passed away and is now in some other dimension, reverting to his easy-going demeanor after his competitive battle with ALS—maybe sharing baseball stories with Lou Gehrig.

Dozens of my former players continued their baseball playing at four-year colleges or in professional baseball. Two of my former players went into professional careers in entertainment as comedians (if that says anything about me as a baseball coach). **Darrell Hammond** came out of Melbourne High School and showed some potential as an outfielder with occasional power at the plate. Decades later Darrell was a long-running comedian on the television show "Saturday Night Live." That comedic talent was evident when he was a player at BCC. I can recall post-game van trips when Darrell would tell jokes and do impersonations. I can remember thinking that this guy had some genuine talent. The only times that I heard him performing in the vans were when we were travelling home after wins. We would travel in two vans, and Darrell would migrate to the other van to do his performances, if we had lost. I wasn't in the mood for comedy, if we had just lost a game.

Mike Cash came from Marietta, Georgia. He was a slick-fielding second baseman. His older brother, Ron Cash, was a standout at rival Manatee Community College. Ron went on to play at Florida State University and made it to the major league level with the Detroit Tigers for two years. I recruited Mike and was able to get him to come to Brevard by offering him out-of-state tuition and textbooks—a partial scholarship. Partial scholarships (no room and board) were all that I could offer, because of our limited baseball budget. Basketball and golf athletes were receiving full scholarships at BCC, so our baseball program was operating on the "third teat down," if you know what I mean. Mike was aware that his older brother, Ron, had received a full ride at the better funded baseball program at Manatee Community College. Mike would often express to me the frustration of the baseball program having a lesser status than other sports at BCC. Jim Oler, the basketball coach and **Floyd Horgen**, the golf coach had richer financial resources than I could acquire for baseball. Our athletic budget was funded for travel and equipment expenses, but the rule was "every coach for himself" in raising funds for more expanded athletic scholarships. At any rate, Mike performed for us for two years and went on to Georgia Southern College, playing two years there. Mike played a few years of minor league baseball.

Mike had one other concern. He hated school work. On many occasions he would come to my office and express how much he hated the academic side of his BCC experience. The only reason that he was staying at BCC was to play baseball, and he had no interest in pursuing an associate degree or a bachelor's degree. Then he met **Patty**. I don't know why she ended up attending BCC, since she came from Tampa. While the initial attraction was romantic, Patty became a force in coercing Mike to take his academic studies more seriously. Mike transferred to Georgia Southern to play baseball for the iconic college baseball coach, **Ron Polk**. Mike attained his degree at Georgia Southern and married Patty. There are thousands of stories similar to Mike's. He came to college for the "wrong athletic reasons," but in the process changed some priorities and ended up being an academic success. I suspect that Patty had a greater impact on Mike's academic accomplishments than the BCC Baseball program, but we both contributed.

Dave Siegriest was a walk-on catching prospect from Nyack, New York. He had a very likeable personality. He loved our baseball-friendly climate. He loved baseball, and he relished the opportunity to try out for our team. As a freshman, he made the team (barely). I always liked to carry three catchers on the roster, because of the higher risk of injury for catchers. He caught in the bullpen, caught batting practice, and helped load and unload equipment. He acted as if he enjoyed every minute of his Brevard baseball experience, but he didn't play much. After his freshman season, the Kenworthy family was traveling north to work the summer at the Ted Williams Baseball Camp in Lakeville, Massachusetts (to be discussed later). The Siegriest family lived near the Tappan Zee Bridge on our way to the camp, so we arranged for a short visit. When we entered their house, we immediately saw a gigantic portrait of Dave in his BCC baseball uniform. It was apparent that his Brevard experience was meaningful to him. For the first twenty games of Dave's sophomore year, he still sat on the bench. A disciplinary action to one catcher and an injury to another catcher thrust Dave into the starting job, and did he ever capitalize on the opportunity! He performed well defensively as a catcher and literally carried us with his bat for the duration of our season. Granted, we had a mediocre year in our conference play and did not qualify for the state tournament that year, but I will always remember Dave's accomplishments for our final 25 games of that season.

Dave went on to college and became a very successful high school baseball coach in the Nyack area. I was not surprised. Pancreatic cancer attacked Dave a few years ago and ended up killing him. I had the opportunity to have a couple of telephone conversations with Dave before he passed away. His likeable personality, his persistence, his love of baseball, his love for coaching, and his love for his players were very evident to the end.

Dave was a sophomore my final year of coaching in 1980. Another sophomore that year was shortstop **Kevin Bates** from Logan, West Virginia. They both were walk-ons who were drowning in the depth charts as freshmen and worked their way up to have successful years at Brevard.

They both had personable dispositions and great work habits. Kevin went to the University of Oklahoma on baseball scholarship and played some professional baseball. Kevin had an uncle who lived in Melbourne, and that was his attraction to Brevard Community College—Melbourne Campus. I would assess Kevin as perhaps the best defensive shortstop that I had in my 12 years of being a head coach. For this reason, I feel guilty when I sometimes misrepresent my last shortstop (Kevin). I have a propensity for trying to achieve a "cheap laugh" sometimes. If I witness someone dropping something or mishandling something, I would remark, "I retired from coaching, because my shortstop had hands like that." I apologize to Kevin for that comment.

Another reason that Dave and Kevin stand out in my memory is that I could appreciate their accomplishments, since I too was a walk-on as a Florida Gator. I spent thousands of hours (over twelve years as a head coach) traveling and being on the phone, trying to lure baseball prospects to play baseball for Brevard. I could essentially offer tuition scholarships and supply some textbooks (no room and board) to attract talent. It was always a challenge to look at a 17-year old player from high school and try to project how dedicated to academics and baseball that player was. Looking back at my track record for selecting the best players deserving baseball scholarships, I would say that I failed more than I succeeded. One reason for this failure rate may be that I never promised a prospect a starting job, while recruiting him. So many of the upper-tier players that I recruited were not accustomed to having to compete for a spot in the starting lineup, and they weren't willing to handle that scenario. The avenue was always open to walk-ons trying out, like Dave and Kevin.

Ernie Rosseau's father guaranteed that his son loved only baseball—nothing else. He lived and breathed baseball, and baseball was his whole life. Many fathers of high school prospects that I recruited said the same thing about their kids, but the fathers either didn't know their kids or they were lying. Most nineteen year old baseball players found ways to participate in extra-curricular activities (some of which could be considered irresponsible activities) that would sometimes get them in trouble. Young Ernie, a graduate of nearby Satellite High School, was all baseball. He wanted to learn everything possible about baseball to enhance his skills. He was a centerfielder with exceptional running speed. At BCC he was a good hitter with the ability to drop down drag bunts to enhance his batting average. He was mostly a singles hitter without power, but he was a pest who could get on base and wreak havoc on the opposition with his base running skills. Ernie played his four-year college ball at the University of South Alabama under the tutelage of former National League infielder, Eddie Stanky. Stanky was referred to as "the brat" during his playing days, because he approached baseball in an aggressive manner. I was told that Stanky was responsible for the re-writing of a few rules in the major league rulebook, because of his creative antics. Ernie developed the same aggressive mindset as Stanky. After South Alabama, Ernie was drafted by the St. Louis Cardinals organization and was successful at the minor league Class A level for a few years. Throughout his minor league playing experience, he would attempt to "pick the brains" of many of the minor league Cardinals managers and coaches. If a pitching coach was working with some pitchers, he would eavesdrop to learn all he could about pitching. Ernie was eventually released by the Cardinals, but he had acquired a huge knowledge base of the many aspects of the game of baseball.

I encouraged Ernie to pursue his master's degree, if he wanted to become a community college baseball coach/physical education instructor like me. After helping me on a part-time basis and infusing tenacity and intensity into our baseball program during a couple of his minor league years, Ernie received his degree and became my assistant in the fall of 1979. I resigned as baseball coach a year later and recommended Ernie as my replacement. Ernie went on to be the baseball coach at BCC for the next three decades and proved to be an astute student and teacher of the game, leading Brevard to two Florida state championships along with two trips to the NJCAA World Series in Grand Junction, Colorado.

In 1972 the Brevard baseball program was moved from the Cocoa Campus to the Melbourne Campus about 30 miles south. My health and physical education teaching responsibilities also were moved to the brand new Melbourne Campus, which consisted of three buildings, an unpaved parking lot, acres of pine trees, and the promise of a baseball field to be constructed on campus. The field was completed in 1975. For two years we played games wherever we could find baseball fields. We practiced wherever we could find cleared land; essentially we were a homeless base-ball team. This situation forced me to be creative and flexible. During the 1973 and 1974 seasons we practiced at Wickham Park, a recreation area over a half mile from the campus. Wickham Park had two lakes with picnic cabanas and pavilions; the park also had two crude, poorly maintained soft-ball fields. We practiced at the softball fields. The recreation department allowed me to have some clay hauled in, so that I could construct two bull-pen pitching mounds. Every day the team would meet outside the locker room on the Melbourne Campus, and we (including me) would jog as a team the half-mile distance to the softball fields and begin our practice. After practice we jogged back to the Melbourne Campus as a team. The only person who could drive to the practice field at Wickham Park was the team manager, hauling our equipment. Everyone else ran. I rationalized that the runs would help to build stamina, and we were making the best of a bad situation (a quality that I suspect I inherited from my mother, Lois). The players thought that I was crazy. The recollection of our jogging to practice makes me think of one former player, **Marshal Harper**.

Marshal may have been the best baseball athlete that I ever coached. He signed with the Chicago White Sox and played a few years in their mi-nor league system. Marshal would sprint the half-mile plus distance to Wickham Park and back, leaving his teammates (including me) way behind him. Years later, former players told me why he ran so fast. Marshal would get to the practice field way ahead of his teammates so that he could sneak a few puffs of a cigarette. His former teammates also intimated that some-times marijuana was involved. When Marshal enrolled at BCC, I gave him a pep talk about trying real hard in the classroom. Marshal was not academically-inclined. I was convinced that Marshal tried his best to suc-ceed during the first semester of his freshman year, but the academic ability was not there. I encouraged Marshal to enroll in our vocational program, acquiring experience in BCC's building construction program. Granted, I wanted to keep Marshal eligible to play baseball, but in the process, Marshal picked up potential vocational skills. After BCC and professional baseball, Marshal started a window washing business. Ironically, two of Marshal's former BCC teammates had received their bachelor's degrees and were having difficulty getting employment in their field of study. Marshal hired them as window washers for his company for a few months. On the baseball field, Marshal was a key player on our "Cinderella" 1975 team. Many years ago Marshal died in a one-car accident, living life on the edge all the way to the end.

Another major player on that 1975 team was **Bruce Bochy**, who decades later became Brevard baseball's "poster boy." When the baseball program was transferred to Melbourne in 1972, I attempted to establish a relationship with the South Brevard baseball community by making myself visible. I was asked to speak at some end-of-year youth baseball banquet in Melbourne. More than one person at that banquet told me about a 15-year old catcher, who was already big in stature and was sure to grow some more. They were talking about Bruce Bochy. Bruce was a year younger than most of his classmates, as a senior at Melbourne High School, making him somewhat of a "sleeper" as a baseball prospect. I offered him a tuition scholarship to play baseball at BCC—one of only two baseball scholarship offers he had received. Bruce chose to come to Brevard.

As a freshman, Bruce obviously had potential to be a good college catcher. Realizing this, I still made a questionable decision. I had a returning catcher who had proved to be a solid defensive catcher as a freshman the year before. This returnee had quick reactions behind the plate and was successful throwing out potential base-stealers. In a move to put my best talent on the field, I made the decision to play Bruce at first base for his freshman year and keep the returnee behind the plate. Bruce was not particularly happy with that decision. I didn't expect him to like it, but he played first base with occasional catching assignments most of that freshman year. Bruce assumed the starting catcher role as a sophomore. He also assumed the unofficial and intangible role of team leader. Maybe it was his stature; he was the tallest player on the team, had big and slow feet and a large head (I had to special order a batting helmet for him). Even though he wasn't excessively talkative, his teammates gravitated to "Boch." Players often turned to Boch to observe his reaction to a particular situation and followed his lead. Decades later the San Francisco Giants would have a run of World Series successes, and experts in major league baseball were crediting field manager, Bruce Bochy, as being especially adept at handling personnel and maximizing the team's potential. As I look back, those leadership qualities were in their early manifestations in 1975.

Bruce could hit for power and had a strong throwing arm. As a former catcher, I would spend time working on fundamentals of catching with all of my catchers with an emphasis on footwork. I immediately observed that Boch simply planted his back foot and threw on steal attempts. I wisely chose to not complicate things and did not interfere with his footwork style. Bruce was the anchor on our 1975 Florida Community College Baseball State Champion team. We opened the state tournament against Miami-Dade South Campus, who had speedy twins who were outstanding base stealers. Boch threw out one of the twins trying to steal second base in the first inning of the first game and threw out the other twin a few innings later. Nobody ran on Brevard for the rest of the tournament.

After our successful 1975 season, Bruce was drafted and signed with the Houston Astros organization. Because of a rash of injuries of catchers in the Astros organization, Bruce moved up quickly in the organization and had his major league debut in 1978. He was a major league player for 9 seasons with the Astros, New York Mets, and the San Diego Padres. Bruce stayed on with the Padres as a minor league coach and manager. Bruce was the San Diego Padres field manager from 1995 through 2006, earning Manager of the Year honors in 1996. He led the Padres to the World Series in 1998, losing to the Yankees. Bruce became the manager of the San Francisco Giants in 2007, leading the Giants to World Series Championships in 2010 and 2012. He has earned the respect of the major league baseball community, and he is still an active manager. Many say he could be a candidate for the Cooperstown Hall of Fame as a manager. While I am extremely proud of Bruce's accomplishments and feel fortunate to be known in some circles as "Bochy's former college coach," I am quick to point out that all I can say is that (as a coach) I didn't screw him up too much. Besides, a coaching mentor informed me decades ago not to take too much credit for your players who become successful. If you take too much credit for your successful players, you must also accept responsibility for your former players who did prison time (and I had a few of those).

**Brevard Community College honored its most
accomplished baseball alumnus in 2011. The baseball field
at BCC (now called Eastern Florida State College)
is now known as "Bruce Bochy Field."**

The 1975 state champion team stands out in my memory. I would categorize myself as a better-than-average college coach. Over my twelve years as head coach, Brevard never had a losing season. We qualified for the annual state junior college championship five times. Only eight teams of the 27 baseball programs in the state of Florida qualified for the state tournament each year. Many of the colleges we were competing against were able to offer more attractive scholarship packages to prospects and had better baseball facilities than Brevard. The total coaching experience at BCC was demanding and rewarding. I relished the opportunity to guide young men through their early college years as students and baseball players. While I appreciated the rewards of mingling with so many people in college baseball circles (young student/athletes and their families, other coaches, professional baseball scouts, other baseball lovers, and even umpires), I would dream and aspire to one day actually coach a Florida state championship team. Until May of 1975, I did not really think that goal was attainable.

Going into the 1975 season, I was not overly excited about our prospects for such a successful season. Our primary offensive threat in 1974, **Mark Van Bever**, had transferred to the University of South Carolina as a rising sophomore, since he had an outstanding grade point average. Eligibility rules allowed the immediate transfer and eligibility of community college athletes to four-year colleges, if they had exceptional grades. We had quite a few returning sophomores who had decent, but not standout, freshman seasons. I believe that I have had more talented teams than the 1975 edition, but these guys became a "Cinderella Team." As the season progressed, it became evident that this team had vibrant chemistry. One professional scout remarked that our team stood out from all the other community college teams he had seen, because of our tenacity. I had to go to a dictionary to research the word tenacity. I suspect that Ernie Rosseau had a hand in instilling some of that tenacity. He had helped as my assistant coach that fall and early spring before he reported to spring training with the Cardinals, but credit goes to the players mainly. They made the critical plays defensively. Pitchers got timely outs. Batters got timely clutch hits. Almost every player on the roster contributed in various ways, but many people recognized that it was no coincidence that we were anchored by Bruce Bochy behind the plate. Some athletes seem to be associated with winning teams. We proceeded to win our conference to qualify for the state tournament at Marchant Stadium in Lakeland, Florida. We went through the double-elimination tournament unscathed, defeating more established and better funded baseball programs.

Winning the prestigious state championship was quite an accomplishment, but we needed to defeat Middle Georgia College for the National Junior College Southeast Regional Playoff in order to qualify for the NJCAA World Series in Grand Junction, Colorado. We lost a two-out-of-three series to Middle Georgia, losing two extra-inning games to them while winning big for our only win. The successful season was over.

I remember the scene in the Cochran, Georgia parking lot after we were eliminated. I held back tears and told the team that they would always be special to me for two reasons: I thanked them for teaching me that aggressive teams push themselves to play better than they really are. I also thanked them for letting me be associated as the coach of a state tournament champion. While I appreciated my many baseball coaching experiences over the total of 14 years, I was proud to have been the coach of a state champion. Then we loaded onto the two 15-passenger vans and drove

10 hours to Melbourne. The next day I had to resume recruiting high school prospects. Because of the post-season success, I was way behind in my recruiting for the next year. At this level of coaching, the job never ended.

Over my twelve years of head coaching, two people stood out as supporters of our baseball program. **Art Pollock** was an academic department chairman at the Melbourne Campus, who happened to be an avid baseball fan. Art took an interest in the academic achievements of many of our student-athletes. He was also helpful in promoting Brevard Baseball throughout the school and the community. He was instrumental in publishing promotional brochures each year for several years that were helpful in recruiting high school baseball prospects, and he was helpful in assisting in the salvaging of some players' grade point averages.

Another very helpful supporter of our program was **Christine Suleski**. Christine was a student assistant who later became an academic department secretary, working for Art. Christine was an example of the perfect secretary with an outstanding work ethic. She, too, was a baseball fan who followed Brevard Baseball. She was an expeditious typist who settled for nothing less than a perfect document. Christine assumed all of our baseball program's secretarial and clerical needs, which included correspondence, rosters, schedules, eligibility forms, and any other secretarial tasks that were needed. Many professional baseball scouts and college baseball coaches would remark to me how all my correspondence was neat, concise, and professionally delivered in a timely manner. She made me look more competent and efficient than I really was.

Coaching baseball at the community college level was very demanding. I had to put a great amount of time and energy into striving to "stay ahead" of my players and opposing coaches, at the expense of my own family. I felt that the players were all part of my extended family, and I was responsible for them and their actions. Rightly or wrongly, coaches are often judged by their won-loss record. During certain periods of the baseball season (and off-season), I spent much more time with my players than with my family members. Gloria had to pick up much of the slack around our house during my coaching days. There is a story about one of my coaching colleagues that many coaches can understand and relate to.

I had met **Joe Walsh** at the Ted Williams Camp. We coached together there for a couple of years. Joe went on to be a successful baseball coach at Harvard for several years. Like many coaches, he put his heart and his soul into his team and his coaching duties. Sadly, Joe passed away a couple of years ago. I read an account of some of his players' memories of his time as a coach. On one particular day the team had played terribly, and Joe was chewing them out after the game. "Your lackluster play makes me question why I am coaching here. I could be spending more time with my three daughters at home, rather than wasting my time with you guys." After Joe had calmed down, a player spoke up, "Coach, don't you have four daughters?" Joe replied, "You might be right."

In 1980, after 14 total years of doing the baseball coaching gig, I decided that I had coached in this setting long enough. There was no pressure to terminate me as a coach (that I was aware of). It is possible that I was experiencing the proverbial "burnout." I have already described the many and varied demands of the job. Up until this point, I had spent much of my adult life on a baseball field, conducting baseball business in my office, at home, and on the road. While I sincerely loved the whole community college baseball scene, I felt that 14 years of this activity was enough for my lifetime. In May of 1980 I submitted my resignation as baseball coach, requesting that I still be retained by BCC as Assistant Professor of Health and Physical Education. At first I was told that I had to resign as a faculty member also. For a short period of time, I thought that I was going to be fired. After a series of meetings, it was determined that I could remain on the faculty without having to coach baseball. An era ended.

JACKGLO'S OFFSPRING

Laci and Russ together with Shannon below.

I HAVE ALREADY expounded on the fact that the marital team of Jack and Gloria (aka JACKGLO) was (and is) a relationship of opposites who had (and have) very little in common with each other. But, in spite of our divergent interests and backgrounds, we managed to bring into this world three lives that represent our greatest accomplishments. Our modest goal was to hopefully produce, nurture, and develop responsible adults. As young, inexperienced, bungling parents, we lacked confidence that we knew what we were doing. Raising responsible adults seemed a very lofty, almost unattainable goal during their formative years. Many can relate that kids can drive you crazy, if you let them. They will push you to the limit. My experiences at BCC displayed to me the many and varied things that can go wrong in the lives of 19 year-old college students—lack of ambition, drug and alcohol abuse, unwanted pregnancies, automobile accidents, family discord, knucklehead decisions. The list could go on. I expected that my kids were not immune to these negative outcomes, and that we would most assuredly have to deal with them. My consistent prayer when they were teenagers was that they would just not screw themselves up too catastrophically, accepting the fact they will make some bad decisions. After all, I remember making a few hundred bad decisions myself, as a teenager.

Before I begin relating the wild ride of raising our three kids, I can unequivocally declare that Russell, Shannon, and Laci far exceeded any expectations I had for them. They succeeded at college. They appear to have acquired upstanding, principled spouses. They appear to be doing all the things responsible adults do. Maybe the greatest testament to their success as adults is that I feel that our five grandchildren are very fortunate to have the parents and family environments that they have. I cannot analyze why Russell, Shannon, and Laci turned out the way that they did. Gloria and I witnessed several of our friends living nightmare scenarios as parents. We escaped those situations. I suspect that one trait that has helped them through adult things like marriage, parenting, being an employee, and just generally living in a stressful world was their sense of humor. Ken and Lois left me with a legacy of laughter, and I like to think that JACKGLO progeny have acquired that trait from me.

Russell Damon Kenworthy came into the world in December of 1968 with a prolonged introduction. Gloria was in labor for 20 hours with

Russell. The plan was that he would affectionately be called "Russ," but with his preponderance for being in some sort of trouble frequently, the name "Russell" evolved. He was a colicky baby, which meant that he was irritable and cried incessantly, even though he was considered a healthy infant otherwise. Pediatricians believe that the non-stop crying actually helps lung and rib cage development. Future medical tests have indicated that Russell did in fact have huge lungs and rib cage. Russell's colic meant that JACKGLO were irritable and sleep-deprived also. We really don't remember Russell's first walking steps. He went from crawling to running, by-passing the walking stage as a toddler. While Russell was in the first grade, Gloria and I had an opportunity to view him and two other students in a small group learning activity. Videotape technology was just being introduced in education in the early 1970's. In the video recording, the teacher was presenting a simple lesson at a round table with three children, one of whom was Russell. While the other two students were attentively sitting and dutifully working on their learning task, Russell was in constant motion circling the table and crawling under the table. On Russell's first day of formal public education, he received a paddling for climbing on a toilet stall (corporal punishment was then allowed by the school principal). "Is this a precursor to his academic future?" JACKGLO asked themselves. Realizing that almost all first-time parents are overwhelmed by this addition to their marriage, we felt that we were in for quite an adventure with Russell—and we were right.

JACKGLO were aware that Russell really deserved to have a sibling, but we were not sure if we could survive another high-energy kid. Reluctantly, Gloria put the birth control pills on the shelf for a while—and in time became pregnant. She tells me that her pregnancy with Shannon was relatively easy. The pregnancy even improved Gloria's bowling average. We were in a bowling league at the time; and, as Gloria's belly grew and her center of gravity changed, her bowling scores continued to improve. Late in the pregnancy, Gloria went for a routine visit to the obstetrician's office and was told that she was in early labor. She was instructed to check herself into the hospital, which was across the street. She called me at BCC from the doctor's office to tell me to go home to get her suitcase and meet her at the hospital. I pleaded with her that I really needed to administer a test in the next half hour before I could get the suitcase. That event was one of the 500,000 times (and still counting) that I have made Gloria mad. I gave the test, went to the house and then to the hospital. Within a couple of hours, **Shannon Elizabeth Kenworthy** was born—on June 3, 1971. It should be mentioned that fathers had no significant role in the actual childbirth process in those days. Expectant fathers could stay in the designated "labor room" until it was time for the delivery, at which time we were relegated to the waiting room to drink coffee and smoke cigarettes and wait for the doctor to come and reveal the gender of the baby (prenatal ultra sound technology was not prevalent then either). The delivery was slick and quick, and the hospital stay was shorter than the norm in the early 1970's (and less expensive). In summary, Shannon was easy. JACKGLO's wedding anniversary was the day after Shannon's birth, and all I had to do for the anniversary was to purchase some roses in the hospital gift shop—and they were on sale for half-price on June 4, 1971. Shannon was introduced to her brother, Russell, on the third day of her life. A few months later, Ken and Lois came to visit us in Merritt Island. Ken enjoyed taking 8 mm. moving pictures of his many grandchildren. Many years later we had the opportunity to view this collection of Grampa's movies that had been converted to DVD's. Included in a DVD is a scene of Russell (about 3 years old) running around a playpen with Shannon (about 6 months old) sitting inside the playpen. Russell is attempting to touch (or punch) Shannon, as he continues to circle the playpen. It is evident that Shannon had learned at an early age that if she stayed exactly still in the middle of that playpen, Russell could not reach her—a principle of geometry. It is no coincidence that in later years Shannon would develop a propensity for mathematics.

The next two years proved that Shannon was noticeably easier to nurture than Russell had been. Whereas, JACKGLO were considering that Russell would be an only child two years before; we were now unsure about having a third child. During the process of uncertainty, **Laci Renee Kenworthy** appeared on the scene on July 11, 1973. As an infant, Laci contracted salmonella. Since Gloria was incapacitated with a post-childbirth surgery, I was especially bonded to the newborn Laci for a few weeks.

To this day, Laci has tired of my corny anecdote that she should be eternally grateful to her sister, Shannon. If Shannon had not been such a low-maintenance baby, there would never have been a third child—there would have been no Laci Kenworthy. Gloria suggested the name, and we decided to spell it with an "i." This meant that her name has been chronically misspelled throughout her life. Laci has taken the misspelling in stride. In fact, I suggest that her often-misspelled name has contributed to her self-confidence. I feel that she handles life's challenges in a courageous, intrepid, and adventurous way. If Laci had been a boy, the name was going to be "Deron." Gloria and I had an agreement that while we would both participate in naming our kids, the final decision would be hers for the girls and mine for the boys. Russell Damon Kenworthy's name was inspired by two southeastern Massachusetts athletes that I followed as a kid—Russ Gibson was a catcher from Fall River who had a short career as a major leaguer with the Boston Red Sox in the late 60's—and Damon Rivard was a star high school football player for Somerset High School in the early 50's whom I didn't know, but thought that he had a neat name (would you say that I am sports-obsessed?). Sitting in the waiting room at the hospital on July 11, 1973, I still had not determined a potential boy's name. Reading the sports section of the local newspaper, I researched which major leaguers had made the headlines that day. A major league baseball player, Deron Johnson, had three hits, including two home runs for the Oakland Athletics on July 10 (again, would you say that I am sports-obsessed?). But, Laci Renee prevailed, not Deron.

I can recall several family anecdotes.

On one occasion, I was alone with all three kids: Russell about nine, Shannon about six, and Laci about four. Gloria was not there, which was a good thing. Shannon presented me with a question. "How do babies get in mommies' bellies?" I was dumbfounded; I had to collect my thoughts about what to say. I was aware that some parenting gurus were advocating that you answer in a truthful and forthcoming manner. Being careful with the wording, I said something to the effect that daddies did something with mommies that caused a baby to grow in the mommies' bellies. Nine-year-old Russell laughed and said, "That's not the way it happens." I said, "Okay, Russell, you tell me how babies get in mommies' bellies." He couldn't come up with an explanation. I remember making a sardonic comment that what I said was true, "but that if you don't believe me, you will just have to learn the birds and the bees on the streets." Decades later, none of them remember this dialogue; but I do.

Consistent with her low maintenance demeanor, Shannon was an obedient child, and she displayed this trait during a BCC baseball game. During our 1975 state championship season, we had a pretty nasty brawl on the baseball field with the Hillsborough Community College baseball team. Late in the game, freshman **Dave Lillemon** tripled with the bases loaded to give Brevard a four-run lead. The third run to score was the aforementioned Marshal Harper. As he crossed home plate, the Hillsborough catcher elbowed Marshal in the ribs out of frustration. Marshal was not a troublemaker, but he was not one to take that elbow without a response. Marshal and the catcher started to wrestle, and players from both benches came out. A full-scale donnybrook erupted. Gloria was at the game with four year-old Shannon and two year-old Laci. Gloria's rule to Shannon was that she could go out to see her daddy, when the players from both teams came together (meaning when players and coaches were shaking hands at the completion of the game). Seeing the two teams "coming together," obedient Shannon found her way to the dugout gate in the midst of the several skirmishes all over the field. As I was attempting to break up the various fights, I saw Shannon approaching the out-of-control melee. Infielder **Mike Gallagher** interrupted his pugilistic activity to pick up Shannon and hand her over to Gloria on the other side of the fence. He then resumed fighting.

The umpire suspended the game, declaring Brevard the winner; police arrived to maintain order. As a coach, I am not proud of this event, but Hillsborough was completely out of control; and our players were involved to protect our own teammates. Most importantly, Shannon was unscathed and was instructed that the players had to be shaking hands for her to go onto the field to see her daddy.

Living seven miles from the Atlantic Ocean, Russell showed a little interest in surfing for a couple of years. One Easter, fourteen year-old Russell informed us that he was going surfing, and he couldn't attend church on that morning. JACKGLO did not force their kids to attend church every Sunday, but Christmas and Easter were mandatory. Russell insisted that all his friends were going surfing, and the waves were going to be real good on Easter morning. I reluctantly made a compromise with him.

St. John's Episcopal Church had 8 and 10 a.m. services that Easter. If he wanted to surf, he could go to the 8 a.m. service with me and I would drive him out to the beach after the service. Russ and I went to church, and I drove him out to the beach with his surfboard after church. I got home about 9:30, as the girls were getting ready for the later service. Since I had nothing else to do, I decided to go to church with Gloria and the girls. During the service, I went up to the communion rail to receive communion for the second time in one morning. As **Father Ned Bowersox** prepared to hand me the communion wafer, he paused and leaned over me and said, "You must have done a lot of sinning in the last two hours."

When Shannon was a senior in high school and Laci was a sophomore, the senior prom was approaching. Both girls were planning to attend the Eau Gallie High School Prom. There was a rumor spreading around town that there were fourteen conceptions that occurred on prom night the previous year at the Eau Gallie High Prom, resulting in premature families, adoptions, or abortions. This rumor couldn't be substantiated, but I suppose it was possible. Parents of teenage girls can relate that at that age, their daughters are fully functioning baby-making factories. The rumor terrorized me. Then Shannon and Laci informed me that all their female friends were going to be spending prom night at a motel and requested permission to stay the night also. Gloria put the decision in my hands. I told the girls that I had to think about it a while. After a week of pondering, I tried to analyze how to resolve this dilemma. Two prominent concerns surfaced in my mind, and I made my decision. I informed them that just because only girls were allegedly staying at the motel didn't mean that boys were not going to also show up. I agreed to allow them to spend the night, but that there would be two rules: 1) don't get pregnant. 2) don't get in a car with a drunk driver. I was later told that "Jack's two rules" were renowned among several students at Eau Gallie High School for a time.

Russell was very active in sports, as he was growing up (imagine that)—mostly football, basketball, and baseball. He was a pretty good high school football player and an exceptional high school baseball catcher. He went to BCC for his first two years and played baseball for Ernie Rosseau. He played for a state champion team in 1989 that went all the way to the NJCAA World Series in Grand Junction, Colorado.

Getting to Grand Junction was my goal every year that I coached, and I fell short of that goal. It was a thrill for me to attend that event as a parent of a player. He accepted a partial baseball scholarship to Valdosta State College in Georgia and played there for a year. Russell ultimately finished his degree at the University of Florida. He has been a certified athletic trainer, treating athletic injuries for various high schools in Florida and Mississippi.

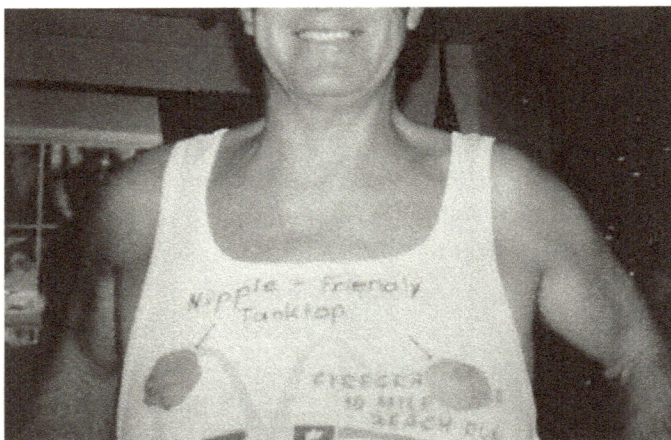

A unique Christmas present from my kids one year. My apologies for the exposed body parts.

Shannon and Laci were the instigators for a Christmas gift that I received one year. Almost every year, I would participate in a half-marathon (13.1 miles) in Orlando in early December. For really long runs, I would attain some discomfort with my nipples. Most shirts then were either made of cotton or a cotton/polyester blend. For runs longer than five miles the shirts would get sweaty and subsequently heavier. Over a period of time and miles, the wetter and heavier fabric would cause abrasion-type irritation to the nipples that would potentially become very sensitive and painful, sometimes resulting in bleeding. The day after one of these half-marathons, the girls were inquiring what I wanted for Christmas. I suggested a "nipple-friendly" running tank top. Around the early 1990's shirt textile technology was producing material that was lighter and wicked moisture adequately, so that the nipples and other body parts wouldn't be so easily irritated. On

Christmas morning I opened my gift from the girls. It was an old cotton tank top that I had received years earlier from a previous race in which I had participated. Two holes had been cut in the chest area of the shirt, about where my nipples would be located. There was writing on the shirt that stated that it was a "nipple-friendly tank top." In a separate gift, I received a legitimate tank top made with the modern and trendy moisture-wicking material.

Shannon and Laci got along with each other fine, in spite of the fact that they were different in many ways. It is amazing that siblings can turn out so differently, even though they were created through the same genetic mix. As years progressed, Shannon showed competence in math and the ability to use good logic in her day to day challenges. Laci didn't. But, Laci displayed the ability to express her thoughts verbally and in writing. Gloria, being a teacher, heard of some studies that were conducted in the 1980's that indicated that some people utilize the right side of their brain more prominently, while others use the left side of their brain more in the learning process. The studies suggested that people who were left-brained were more logical, analytical, and objective and were attracted to math and the sciences. Right-brained people were more intuitive, thoughtful, and subjective and showed more interest in the creative arts. Gloria found a test that would indicate which side of the brain certain students would primarily use in problem solving. Guess what? Test results of the girls revealed that Shannon was as far "left-brained" as Laci was "right-brained."

An illustration of these divergent traits occurred a few years later when both girls were college students. I was constructing a walkway in front of the house. While both girls were present one day, I asked Shannon to do some math for me. I specified that my walkway was 40 feet long and 4 feet wide. I was installing some stepping stones that were 18 inches in diameter, and they would be centered every 24 inches. After I installed the stepping stones, I wanted to use small river rocks to fill in the rest of the walkway 3 inches deep. I asked Shannon, "How many cubic feet of river rocks do I need to purchase?" As Shannon was punching numbers into her multi-functional calculator, Laci spoke up, "I don't understand the problem. You go to the store and buy river rocks. If you didn't get enough, you go back and buy some more."

All three of our kids went to Brevard Community College for their first two years of college. Shannon never enrolled in a class that I taught, but Russell and Laci did. I didn't even realize that Russell had registered for one of my Health Analysis and Improvement classes. On the first day of class I entered the classroom and went to the podium in the front of the room. Sitting right in front of me in the first row was Russell with his notebook out, frantically taking notes of almost everything I was saying. I found this quite bizarre, since Russell went through his teenage years leaving the impression that his father was not too smart. Russell was a conscientious college student, eventually graduating from the University of Florida with honors.

Laci enrolled in a First Aid and Safety class that I taught. For some reason, I thought it best that we not reveal that I was Laci's dad for the first few weeks, and then reveal it later. I instructed Laci that when I called roll, I would call her "Laci Kennedy." Some of her classmates knew I was her dad; some did not know. We were practicing CPR and choking skills during the second week of the term. I was conducting the class on the gymnasium floor. The class was instructed to break up into groups of two and practice simulated choking skills on each other. With the class roster in my hand, I told the class that I would be floating around the room to make suggestions on the performance of their skills. And, if any of them displayed perfect competency, I would check them off on the roster for that particular skill.

Laci was paired off with some guy whom she didn't know. The guy was understandably hoping to get checked off right away. He made a couple of mistakes and a couple of omissions, as he was simulating choking skills on Laci. I explained that he needed to work on his skills some more and I will check him off at a later time. After I left the area, the guy told Laci, "He looks like he enjoys being an a**hole." Within a couple more weeks it was revealed to the whole class that Laci was, in fact, my daughter. Upon learning this, Laci's CPR partner humbly apologized to Laci, regarding his earlier comment about what I enjoy. Laci told me later how embarrassed he felt.

Shannon was the proverbial middle child, when it was time for her to get on the school bus for her first day of school. Getting on the school bus for the very first time should be a major, ceremonial milestone. I had gone to work; and while Gloria was busily and frantically devoting attention to 7-year old Russell and 3-year old Laci, Shannon went to where she was told that the bus would stop and boarded the bus with no hoopla. A few minutes later Gloria realized that Shannon was gone. Shannon was easy to bring up.

Many years later, Shannon was about to receive an award at a Brevard Community College awards ceremony. Gloria and I were there to proudly witness her receiving this award. About 25 people were receiving awards that day, and Shannon was the 20th in line. After the 19th student was awarded, a campus security officer appeared on the stage to inform every-one that there was a bomb scare and to vacate the building immediately. Shannon missed out on the glory that day, as the proverbial forgotten mid-dle child.

Shannon's wedding day was badly timed. Shannon married **Chris Dexter** in Fort Worth, Texas about five weeks after the fateful September 11, 2001. Most friends and family were from places not in Texas, which meant that almost everyone had to fly to attend the wedding at a time when most people were wary of flying. A handful of the invitees cancelled plans to attend the wedding, but a remarkable number of their friends and family did attend. All three of our kids had an abundance of friends. Over their school years, I can remember quite a few parent-teacher conferences, dur-ing which time Gloria and I were informed that our children were very so-cially adept.

Speaking of weddings, Laci was the first to marry. I was informed by Laci that I was not to cry at her wedding. So I heeded her mandate. Shannon's wedding was next, and I again forced myself to "man up" and not cry. Russell was the last of the offspring to marry. I am embarrassed to say that I succumbed to tears at my son's wedding. Russell grew up with so much more drama than his sisters; Russell seemed to have more crises than his sisters; Russell seemed to have more emotional high and low points than his sisters. Through all this, Russell graduated from college with honors, became a certified athletic trainer with a courageous and admirable work ethic, and was starting married life with a neat girl, Beth. Watching my daughters participate in the wedding in a dignified manner and realizing that Russell had come so far, I felt a wave of pride for my kids and couldn't hide the fact that I was tearing up. All three had become "responsible adults."

Russell married **Beth Carney** from Long Beach, Mississippi. Beth is an elementary school teacher in the Mississippi Gulf Coast area. Russ (we call him Russ more now that he is a responsible adult and is in less trouble with us) is a certified athletic trainer for a local high school. Russ and Beth have two kids, **Nathan** and **Amelia**.

Shannon met her husband, Chris Dexter, while she was getting her master's degree at Florida Institute of Technology in Melbourne, Florida. She kept referring to him as "Dexter," so I assumed that his first name was "Dexter." A couple of years passed before I learned his full name. Chris is a national sales representative, selling diesel fuel to large trucking companies. They provided us with one grandson, **Joshua**. Ironically, Shannon teaches math at Brevard Community College. I tell people that I taught courses like weight training, bowling, tennis, and team sports; while, Shannon teaches courses like algebra, statistics, and calculus. As Shannon was initially interviewing for a teaching job at BCC, I suggested that she mention to the interviewing committee that her father was on the faculty at BCC for 30 years. I had retired from BCC 12 years earlier. She said that she did mention my name at an appropriate time during the interview, and nobody had ever heard of me. While my ego suffered a setback, I was proud that Shannon received her job on her own merits.

While Laci was our youngest, she was the first of our offspring to get married, to have a child, and to possess a mortgage. After getting some high school boyfriends out of her system, she introduced us to a great guy with many positive attributes. Laci met **Dean Carroll** in the back of a grocery store garbage dumpster. They were both employed at the store. Dean was on active duty in the Air Force at nearby Patrick Air Force Base. He was a breath of fresh air after some of Laci's aforementioned acquaintances in high school. Dean picked up computer skills while he was in the Air Force and is a lead systems administrator for a large manufacturing firm in Radford, Virginia. Dean discharged from the Air Force about the time they were getting married. I remember the wedding and reception well. Just before the couple were leaving in a Chevy S-10 pickup truck for their new home in the hills of southwest Virginia, Laci asked me if I could ship all of their wedding presents to Virginia. That was a wedding expense I didn't foresee. **Jenna**, our first grandchild, was born in 1999. She was born within days of my father, Ken, passing away. I consider Jenna as being my "replacement person" for Ken. Ten years after Jenna was born, another daughter, **Dani**, came into the world. Laci is an elementary school reading specialist in Dublin, Virginia.

Occasionally I read some sociological/psychological studies that hint that parents love some of their offspring more than others (I can remember when one daughter would say that something was unfair, and I would jokingly say that was because the other daughter was my favorite). I can unequivocally state that I love all three of our kids equally for different reasons. I am also proud of their accomplishments for different reasons. Their variety is refreshing. Jack and Gloria spent a good part of two and a half decades making thousands of decisions, hoping we were doing the right things in raising our kids. We look at our results with pride. One of my most cherished Christmas presents (other than the "nipple-friendly tank top") was a plaque from Laci. The plaque read, "Parents leave their children two things; one is roots; the other wings."

Laci, Gloria, Jack, Shannon, Russ in the late 1990's.
They turned out great!

TED WILLIAMS CAMP

IN SOME PEOPLE'S minds **Ted Williams** was the most popular and most accomplished player to put on a Boston Red Sox uniform. He played with the Red Sox from 1939 until 1960, but World War II and the Korean Conflict military commitments prevented him from producing even more impressive offensive statistics. Toward the end of Ted's playing career, two brothers (**Bernie and Al Cassidy**) and one brother-in-law (**Lester Warburton**) met with Ted to form a summer baseball camp for kids aged 7 to 17. They each would hold one-fourth ownership in the endeavor. The major emphasis of the camp program was obviously baseball. In the early years other activities and sports were included in the program, but by the 1970's the kids' activities only included baseball and time at the waterfront, swimming on Loon Pond. It was a true summer camp with kids staying for two-week and three-week sessions throughout the summer. The campers stayed in rustic cabins and dormitories, and they ate in the mess hall. They practiced and played baseball. They discussed baseball with a minority of the campers being Yankee fans and the majority being Red Sox fans. The camp was set back in the woods in the small town of Lakeville, Massachusetts.

Our family of four (Laci was not born yet) were in Massachusetts during the summer of 1972; visiting my parents, brother Hugh and his family, and sister Joan and her family. Joan's son, **Jack**, was playing summer baseball in Berkley, Massachusetts a few towns away from Lakeville. Since the Berkley team was going to the Ted Williams Camp to play one of the camp teams one Saturday, I thought I would go along to see him play and to witness the camp operation. It was impressive. There were four games being played simultaneously at the baseball complex. I introduced myself to the director, Bernie Cassidy. I mentioned that I might be interested in coaching during a few weeks in the summer. Since most of my family lived within 25 miles of Lakeville, I felt that coaching at Ted Williams Camp might be a good fit with my baseball background. Coaches and their families stayed in individual rustic cabins located in the woods near the lake (Loon Pond) and ate at the mess hall, as part of the pay and benefits package.

I started work at TWC the next year, and I worked there for many summers between 1973 and 1984. While it was pretty hectic, I always looked forward to traveling from Florida to Massachusetts for a few weeks in the summer. The coaching staff consisted of a variety of high school and college coaches from a variety of locations throughout the country. Gloria and I developed friendships with coaches and their wives that we will always cherish. I philosophized that when you have friends that you only see a few weeks a year, you appreciate them more and don't tire of their company. We ate at many of the area restaurants together. The coaches would schedule pizza and beer sessions, talking baseball and other topics (but mostly baseball). When Russell turned seven, he could participate as a camper free of charge. He stayed with the other campers in the dorms and cabins. Shannon and Laci spent hundreds of hours swimming in Loon Pond. We also had much family time during our stays in Massachusetts. I had an abundance of nephews and nieces. Remember, brother Hugh and sister Joan married good Catholics.

Campers came from all over the country and all over the world. The camp tuition was a little pricey. The baseball skill level of the campers and junior staff, ages 16 to 18, wasn't too impressive; but I actually found some players that I convinced to come to Brevard Community College to play baseball. One such player was **John Murphy**, a recent graduate from Boston Latin High School. A sparkplug for our 1974 BCC team was Mark Van Bever, an infielder who was also an exceptional student. Mark's grades were so high that he was eligible to transfer and play immediately as a sophomore at a four-year college. Mark was recruited to play at the

University of South Carolina under former New York Yankee, Bobby
Richardson. I learned that I had lost Mark while I was up in Lakeville, and I
was desperate for another infielder.

John Murphy was planning to attend Northeastern University and live
at home in West Roxbury, Massachusetts. Tuition was extremely expensive
at Northeastern. I sat down with John to do a cost comparison of attending
BCC versus Northeastern. I offered to cover John's tuition and books. We
calculated his room and board expenses and included his cost of two
round-trip airline tickets from Boston to Melbourne, Florida. The result
was that it was much more economical for John to attend BCC. John came
to Brevard and was the second baseman on our 1975 state champion team.
As a sophomore, John had the second leading batting average in the state
(which included 27 junior college baseball programs). Ironically, John also
was recruited to play at South Carolina. Mark and John were starting in-
fielders on a 1977 South Carolina baseball team that were runners-up in the
College World Series held in Omaha, Nebraska.

During the 1960's Ted Williams was very active and involved in the
operation of the camp. He stayed on the grounds and actively coached.
When I began work at TWC, Ted was the manager of the Washington
Senators, which later became the Texas Rangers. Obviously, he was not
able to be at the camp. Within a couple of years, he was terminated as the
Rangers manager. Then Ted spent most of his time fishing in the Florida
Keys with occasional fishing trips to Nova Scotia. Then one day in the late
1970's, Camp Director, Bernie Cassidy, instructed all the campers that they
were to report to their cabins and dorms until further notice. The camp was
buzzing with rumors about what was going on. The word leaked to the
coaches that "Teddy Ballgame" was in fact in Lakeville and was going to
address all the campers and coaches. The atmosphere could be likened to
"The Messiah" himself coming to the Ted Williams Camp. The coaches
and the campers were in awe. While he demonstrated that he was a proud
and egotistical man, Ted showed a fondness to the campers and was very
cordial to all of us coaches and our families.

The camp closed its operation in 1984. All the coaches who had ever
coached at TWC over the years were urged to attend the final closing cere-
monies. I drove up from Florida by myself for the meaningful event. When

I checked into the camp office, I observed an 8-year-old boy in the office who acted as if he owned the place. His name was John Henry Williams, Ted's youngest son. In later years, John Henry devoted much of his time protecting his father's memorabilia. He is most infamously remembered for allegedly being responsible for his father's remains to be frozen in a decapitated state. John Henry mysteriously died shortly after his father passed away.

THE TWILIGHT YEARS
OF KEN AND LOIS

IN THE SUMMER of 1975, I was riding high. I was the winning coach of a state championship community college baseball team. While I was on the receiving end of accolades for winning the state title as a coach, I received a sobering, disturbing phone call from Massachusetts. Lois had been diagnosed with inoperable cancer throughout her abdominal area and had maybe six months to live. She had lived her first seventy years very actively and in an apparently healthy state. The only time that she ever spent in a hospital was to deliver four babies. She was the true matriarch of our family of 4 offspring and 21 grandchildren, the glue that defined the legacy of the Kenworthy family. During her many years at Guantanamo Bay, she was a parental figure to hundreds of people. The Kenworthy family was not accustomed to sickness, and we all had a difficult time accepting and coping with this devastating news. From the moment of the diagnosis, Ken devoted all of his time and energy to helping Lois through this disease. It was evident that all of his care and treatment of Lois was draining Ken. Lois suffered for a year before passing away at the age of 71. She lasted six months longer than the doctor's original prognosis, which was a testament to the extent of Ken's diligent nursing care. We all can reflect on the bonds that we had with our mothers. An older coaching acquaintance of mine pointed out to me that when you lose your mother, you lose the best friend you will ever have in this world. You lose the one who changed most of your diapers and saw you at your worst moments. Lois guided me through my childhood and adolescence. During a discussion on morals and ethics, a friend once asked me how to determine the "right thing to do." After several moments of searching for an answer, I finally concluded that the "right thing to do" was whatever my mother approved of. I am not pretending that I did all the right things, but Lois was my measurement standard.

There are two issues that I still occasionally discuss over Lois' gravestone. I had a pretty extensive collection of baseball bubblegum trading cards as a kid in 1955. When we left for Guantanamo Bay, I was instructed that I could not take my baseball card collection with me. Lois informed my sister Joan to get rid of Jackie's cards, when Joan was preparing to move stuff out of our Milford Road home, which was being sold. The loss of those cards was a sentimental (and financial) blow to me. Also, my mother always taught me to be courteous and respectful to girls—and I was. While that is a virtuous and admirable piece of advice, I sometimes questioned that advice in high school and college. I discovered that some of the girls that I was interested in seemed to be attracted to "the bad boys."

Ken was lost and depressed following Lois' death. He had devoted a lot of heart and energy during Lois' last year of life, trying to make her as comfortable as possible. He and Lois had been married for 47 years (having now been married for 47 years myself, I can appreciate how much heart and energy is required just to survive that period of time as a couple). Ken decided to take a road trip to Florida to visit Frank and me. He was obviously very lonely. He arrived in Melbourne about the time that Gloria and I had purchased a "handy man special" home in need of much repair. I rationalized that I could help divert Ken's depression by putting him to work, installing a new bathroom in our recently purchased house. While I considered this an admirable act of compassion for Ken's situation, I also recognized that we were using and abusing Ken's various mechanical and construction skills for our benefit.

Ken's physiological condition was drained with fatigue from his 13-month stint, nursing Lois. Much of the family was concerned that we may even lose Ken soon. My brother, Hugh, and I had a discussion with Ken about snapping out of his depression. We pointed out to him that there was a multitude of widows out in the field for him to consider as another mate. In his depressed demeanor he answered, "They are mostly old ladies; I would need to find someone with her pilot light still on." After a couple of months Ken returned to his Berkley, Massachusetts, home, which he shared with Joan's family.

Months later Ken announced excitedly to Joan that he had an upcoming date with a nice lady. According to Joan, he was obviously energized and excited about a lady named Marie. On his second date with **Marie Clough** he didn't come home. He returned the next morning for a toothbrush and a few other incidentals and wasn't seen for another day. Ken and Marie became an item as a couple. Marie looked like Lois in many ways. Gloria and I eventually met Marie on a double-date. The scene at a Plymouth, Massachusetts restaurant was bizarre. My father and this other lady were flirting with each other across the table from us. When Ken picked up the dinner roll basket, he asked Marie, "Wanna roll?" Marie winked and answered, "Not now, but maybe later." The remainder of the restaurant date consisted of "grab-a** episodes" and other teenage-like activity. Many months later in Florida, Ken and Marie were at an Italian restaurant with four other family members, when we decided to toast some recently poured wine. Ken urged Marie to recite her special toast. Marie raised her glass and said, "Here's to the girl in the pretty red shoes. She spent all my money and drank all my booze. She's lost her cherry, but that's no sin. She still has the box that the cherry came in." Needless to say, the shock and awe of that toast caused some people to spill their wine. And, needless to say, Ken had found someone with her "pilot light still on."

Ken and Marie were married in 1979 and were married for 20 years. All of our large family agreed that Lois was a tough act to follow, actually an impossible act to follow. While some of Lois' grandchildren probably had a difficult time accepting Marie, the whole family appreciated that Marie brought Ken back to the energetic person that we had all missed the previous two years. Marie embraced the large Kenworthy family and helped to record and acknowledge the birthdays of Ken's 21 grandchildren and around 50 great-grandchildren. Ken and Marie complemented each other. Marie had vision problems, and Ken had hearing problems; but, together they were one "cognitive unit." In their later years together, Marie would often refer to Ken as Horace (Marie's first husband). Ken never knew the difference; he couldn't hear.

**Ken was lost and depressed following Lois' death in 1976. A
year later, Marie (pictured above) brought my father back
to life. Ken and Marie were married for twenty years.
Ken died in 1999; Marie died in 2000.**

Ken and Marie had a home in Taunton, Massachusetts. They purchased a used trailer in a trailer park in Melbourne, Florida (four miles from our home), and became "snowbirds." Every November Ken would drive to Florida to their trailer home, returning to Massachusetts in May. The trip was 1,300 miles one way, and Ken and Marie were well into their eighties. The responsible adult in me was saying that soon I was going to have to intervene and insist that Ken not drive these long distances at his advanced age. At the same time I realized that Ken and Marie valued and cherished their activity and their independence. I chose not to intervene. Instead, I prayed that for every time they took this 1,300 mile trip God would protect others sharing the road with them. My prayer was: if they were to get into an accident, they would be the only ones maimed or killed. After all, they were doing what they wanted to do. While I consider myself a Christian, I am sometimes wary of what to ask for when I pray. I believe that God the Father, God the Son, and God the Holy Spirit have a huge impact on how I live my life and make life's decisions. But, I sometimes have a problem believing that God micro-manages the many and varied events in our life. At any rate, Ken and Marie were able to drive as snowbirds for over 15 years unscathed.

Ken and Marie made their last trip to Florida in November 1998. Ken appeared healthy (as healthy as you can appear as a 91 year-old man). In early January 1999, Gloria and I were preparing to spend a few days at Disney World for the upcoming Disney Marathon. I had seen Ken the night before at his trailer home, and I was concerned that his ankles were quite swollen. His energy was also lackluster. I felt that I needed to check on Ken and Marie before we left town. The next morning his condition appeared to have worsened; he was short of breath. I took him to the emergency room immediately to discover that he was experiencing his first heart attack at age 91. His diagnosis was congestive heart failure, and his prognosis was not good. On that day Ken's life turned to crap, after living almost 92 years of relative health, fulfillment, and happiness. On his third day in the hospital, I witnessed Ken attempting to console 90 year-old Marie. This scene struck me as poignantly strange. The one who will soon die is consoling the one who will survive. Who wins? The person dying or the one left to live alone?

Ken's first heart attack, coupled with a variety of medications caused Ken's cognitive abilities to fluctuate from disorientation to lucidity. During his good periods, his trademark sense of humor remained evident. After a week in the hospital he was transferred to a rehabilitation center. After his admission to the center I was instructed to go to the business center, where I was confronted with paperwork about 4 inches thick. As his medical advocate, I could sign many of the documents; but, I was given a small pile that I had to take to Ken for his signatures. One of those documents was an advanced health care directive or living will. I attempted to explain to my sometimes lucid (sometimes out of touch with reality) father. "This document states that if two physicians diagnose your condition to be terminal, you agree that they not actively perform measures to keep you alive." Ken responded, "I will sign that, and I want one of those physicians to be ..." People in the room were trying to imagine which physician he was attempting to recall. Finally, he remembered, "Jack Kevorkian." Okay, Dad, we got the message!

You could never predict Ken's mental state during his stay in the re-hab center. One of Ken's trademarks throughout his adult life was his ability to recite a poem, entitled "The Clam." Large family gatherings were not complete until "Grampa" stood up and recited this 4 minute-long poem from memory. The poem recalled an Englishman's visit to New England, where he witnessed and described people eating clams. The poem was humorous and especially entertaining when told in a British dialect, as Ken could skillfully perform. Ken learned the poem in 1937, because he had to perform some talent upon his becoming the leader of his Masonic Temple. He never forgot that poem. During a visit to the rehab center one day, I asked if he could give us a performance of "The Clam." To our amazement, he did it. He did it several times during his last two months of life. Most of the time, he didn't know where he was or what was going on, but he could recite "The Clam."

Ken's cardiologist was of Indian descent with a dark complexion. On one occasion, the doctor visited him in his hospital room. The confused Ken beckoned me to come closer and asked me in a subdued voice what the Puerto Rican was doing here. "That's your doctor, Dad." Ken mentioned that he wanted to go back to Massachusetts. He wanted to die in Massachusetts. The doctor informed me that he would approve Ken flying to Massachusetts, but he wanted to conduct some more tests so that he could tweak his medication. Upon learning that he could go north after doing some more tests to tweak his medication, Ken responded, "Tweak my medication; he just wants to get the last Medicare money out of me before I leave."

Brother Frank came up from Miami to help me escort Ken and Marie on a flight to Massachusetts. Ken got his wish and died in Massachusetts within a month. Missing her spouse of twenty years, Marie died a year later. Ken was buried next to Lois in Swansea; Marie was buried in that same plot. Ken is sharing the same earth as his wife of 47 years and his wife of 20 years. I was offered the remaining slot for my burial, but I declined.

Ken (Hugh W.) and Lois were married for 47 years, and
Ken purchased this headstone upon Lois' death in 1976.
Marie's name was added in the early 1990's. Ken offered the
fourth space to me, but I declined. I hope things are
peaceful down there.

THE TRANSITION FROM BASEBALL COACH TO PHYSICAL EDUCATION INSTRUCTOR

MY DECISION TO leave coaching was difficult, but I was able to stay employed at BCC with the exclusive title of physical education instructor (technically I had earned the academic title of "Assistant Professor of Health and Physical Education"). As a coach, physical education faculty member, and a family man; I was spread so thin that I often felt that I was only able to perform in a half-a** manner in all three of those areas. By calculation, I was doing the work of one and a half men. It was a relief to have a little more time to devote to my family. I continued teaching courses in health, first-aid, sports activities and fitness activities. BCC continued to have a significant health/physical education requirement for all of its degree-seeking students. The college had a vast variety of course offerings in this area.

The faculty at the University of Florida's College of Health, Physical Education, and Recreation were effective in instilling in me the importance of fitness and sports for a productive, meaningful, and diversified adult life. Many people make light of "p.e. majors" in college. While I never took the proverbial "Basket Weaving" class in college, there were courses offered in "Fly Fishing" and "Square and Social Dance" at the University of Florida. The premise of our physical education degree curriculum was that students need to be exposed to various sports, recreational, and fitness activities in order to use their leisure time more effectively. I totally bought into this concept. Brevard Community College had a 4 credit-hour health/physical education requirement all 30 years of my time as an assistant professor of health and physical education there, and I was sold on the importance of that requirement. Many BCC students did not share my enthusiasm for the requirement. One of my professional missions as a faculty member was to make my classes interesting, informative, and enjoyable. My goal was to change my students' attitude toward this "archaic, meaningless, and stupid" college requirement. My strategy of relating interesting stories and telling corny jokes changed attitudes in some students, but certainly not all. Having shed my baseball coaching duties, teaching health and physical education classes at the community college level became my primary professional focus.

Using my tennis class syllabus as an example of what I taught, the outline would include: learning skills of the various tennis strokes, tennis etiquette, how to score, strategies with a competitive tournament at the end of the term. A weight training course outline would include: safety guidelines of weight training, physiological principles of resistance training, weight training as an aspect of total fitness, proper technique of specific weight training exercises, weight training exercises and which muscle groups are targeted. In my mind, these informative bodies of knowledge were beneficial to college students' total development in their preparation for a fulfilling adult lifestyle (including their wise use of leisure time).

As years progressed into the mid-1980's, a shift of emphasis occurred with people taking more control of their lifestyle. Studies were indicating that individuals could increase their chances of staying healthy by making wiser choices. We became more aware that we could improve our chances of staying healthy; if we stopped smoking, exercised more, ate more wisely, lost weight, managed our stress more effectively, and were vigilant of signs and symptoms of threatening illnesses and other conditions. Miami-Dade Community College had initiated a course entitled "Health Analysis and Improvement" that stressed all of the healthy lifestyle choices mentioned above. The course at Miami-Dade even utilized computers to assist students in assessing their current status of health and fitness. Students would assess their own body weight, height, percent body fat, blood pressure, resting heart rate, cardiovascular endurance, muscle strength, muscle endurance, and flexibility. Scores for each of these elements of health and fitness were entered into a computer. The computer would analyze all this data and spit out a personalized report that would rate and compare their scores with other students of their age and gender. This technology is not that remarkable in the 21st century, but this computerized report was considered trendy in the 1980's. The course also covered cognitive topics, such as: components of fitness, exercise physiology, nutrition, and stress management. I spent a lot of time developing this course at BCC, using the Miami-Dade model as a guide. The course became an integral part of our health/physical education requirement at BCC in 1984. My observation was that many students came into the class with negative attitudes, but became more interested as the class progressed. After all, the course was really all about each individual student. The various assessments had no bearing on their grade. The purpose of the assessments was for each student to analyze which health/fitness areas were considered good, and which areas required some improvement. I taught an abundance of Health Analysis and Improvement classes my last 12 years at Brevard Community College.

When I was transferred from the Cocoa Campus to Melbourne in 1972, we did not immediately have an indoor gymnasium in which to conduct many of our physical education activity classes. Most of our classes were conducted in an outdoor pavilion. Aerobics was emerging as a popular class in the late 1970's, particularly among the coeds. The only location for these aerobics classes was this outdoor pavilion. These classes, featuring exercising to loud and rhythmic music, became very popular among the female students. The classes also attracted a following of male students who could park their cars in the adjacent parking lot and leer at the scantily-clad coeds dancing to the music. The scheduled days and times of these classes was common knowledge to many of our male student body (and maybe others). Understandably, many of the coeds were uncomfortable with this setting. The physical education faculty anxiously awaited the completion of a new indoor gymnasium in 1980. The architectural plans called for a dedicated room for aerobics classes (and other classes) that provided more privacy from leering spectators. But, things did not work out so well.

As the gymnasium was being completed, the physical education faculty learned that this dedicated room could not be used for its intended purpose. The college had received a federal grant to develop a vocational program in precision sheet metal fabrication, and someone in authority had determined this special room in the newly-constructed gymnasium would be perfect for housing this program. Our popular aerobics classes would be relegated to the wide open gymnasium floor in full view of many and varied people (including leering guys). The sheet metal cutting equipment arrived and was installed in the room. The federal grant also included supplying the potential students with a variety of hand-held metal cutting devices (snips and bolt cutters). Equipment included lab coats with several deep pockets for the students. The program was ready to be launched, but nobody signed up. Frantic for students, the college decided to work with the county correctional institute (prison) to find recently released inmates to train them in metal cutting. This concept sounded good on paper—re-train our less fortunate to give them marketing skills to put them back on the work force.

Within days after the students (ex-cons) began the sheet metal program, theft and vandalism ran rampant in our locker rooms. Some of the lockers had been blatantly cut open with all contents removed. The perpetrators' identity became immediately obvious. These felons felt as if they had died and gone to heaven after being released from prison. They were issued tools and lab coats with deep pockets and were given free reign to our locker rooms. After enforcing certain rules such as no lab coats in the locker room, the theft and vandalism rate abated. I don't remember the sheet metal program lasting too much longer. The room was later assigned to the law enforcement academy. Many years later the aerobics classes were assigned to a dance studio in a nearby building.

As an instructor/professor for 30 years, I felt that I could read students' facial expressions and body language, as an indication of their engagement in the class. I was not always right. I remember one female student who sat in the second row in the middle of the classroom. I had her tagged as someone who resented having to take this stupid class. She appeared expressionless and bored with everything that we were doing in

Health Analysis and Improvement—for all sixteen weeks duration of the class. She received a passing grade. I had her pegged as someone who was just glad that the class was over, feeling that the class was a waste of her time. I happened to see her a year later in the cafeteria, when she came to my table and proceeded to tell me how much she benefitted from the course. The course caused her to examine some of her health and fitness choices and to make positive changes in her life. She raved about the pertinence of the subject matter. I never saw her again, but that was a pleasant surprise. Not wanting to get caught up with myself, I am sure that there were a significant number of students who felt that my classes were a waste of time—and, as evidenced below, a waste of money.

I remember another female student who was missing many classes. I regarded attendance as an important part of the course experience. She appeared to be intelligent, since she was getting "A's" on all of her tests. I tried to design my tests, so that you had to study fairly intensely to get an "A." In spite of her poor attendance, she knew the material. The class met from 12 noon to 12:50 p.m. During a conference with her, I told her that while she obviously knew the material, she had to improve her attendance. Her excuse was that sometimes her work interfered with her ability to make the class. I cut her a little slack on her attendance record, and she received an "A" in the class. A few days after the semester ended, I was reading the local newspaper. The local paper had a section entitled the "Arrest Record," which would list all of the local arrests in Brevard County. I would joke (but I was half-serious) that I read this arrest column, so that I would be one of the first to know if Russ, Shannon, or Laci were arrested. To my surprise, that "A" student appeared in the arrest record. Her charge was prostitution. Then I noted what time she was arrested: 12:24 p.m. So, there was a possibility that she was providing "nooners" during the past semester—during my 12:00 to 12:50 Health Analysis and Improvement class. I can only speculate her dilemma. "Do I attend Mr. Kenworthy's class today or do I make some money?"

As a community college assistant professor, I heard my share of excuses for missing classes. Since this book is an educator's memoir, I should relate to you the most original excuse that I ever heard. Every teacher has a list of wild excuses that have been presented to them. It was a tennis class, when I was teaching at the Cocoa Campus of BCC. The tennis courts were adjacent to a large parking lot. A male student quit attending my tennis class. I had not seen him nor heard from him in 3 weeks. He finally appeared to make his case to stay in the class, in spite of excessive absences. According to him, he and his girlfriend ran away to Georgia to elope. His newly-acquired father-in-law was not happy about the elopement and had vowed to hunt him down and shoot him. "Coach, he knew I was taking this tennis class, and I would have been a sitting duck with this parking lot nearby. So, I stayed in hiding until he cooled down three weeks later."

Toward the end of my teaching career, I noticed that the definition of an acceptable excuse was changing. Students would ask to be excused from class, because they were going on a five-day ski vacation. I would rant that they should plan their vacations around obligations like work or school. I told them that when I was a college student, we would lie and use the dying grandfather excuse.

During my first three years of teaching physical education activity classes, they were segregated by gender. I was teaching all guys. If the class was all male, it was expected that certain things could be said and done during class. If the class was co-ed, certain language and actions had to be curtailed. My first co-ed class was a tennis class. I felt the need to spend some time with the guys to explain that they needed to behave themselves in a gentlemanly manner, since some of their classmates were now "ladies." I spent the first ten minutes of that first co-ed tennis class, addressing the guys about watching their language and acting in a civilized manner. As I was talking to the guys, the girls were informally rallying with each other on the courts over my shoulder. My message to act like gentlemen soon fell on deaf ears, when one of the girls over my shoulder hit a ball into the net and loudly exclaimed, "Sh*t."

In due time all activity classes were co-ed, and I think that was a good trend. One particular co-ed weight training class I was teaching had two attractive girls who were attending the class, but were not officially registered for the class. I was "called on the carpet" by the registrar's office. I was informed that I was to allow only those registered for that class to be attending. It was not fair for those un-registered students to be using the equipment and taking up space, denying those properly registered students full use of the facilities. The next day I informed the girls that they could no longer be in the weight room during the class. I went on to tell them that they were taking up space and depriving those "paying students" of full use of the facilities. As soon as I finished, four guys who were eavesdropping informed me that they didn't care if the girls were taking up space and urged me to let them stay in the class. I chose to let them stay in the class. My argument was the guys' morale would suffer without those girls in the weight room. Did I mention that the girls were attractive?

I enjoyed my teaching. I was sold on the value of the subject matter. I relished observing students' faces respond, when they got engaged in something I was saying. I did have an element of "ham" in me, and teaching gave me that platform to speak in front of a crowd. Not everyone was enthralled with what I had to say. Over a period of 30 years of teaching, I witnessed hundreds (maybe thousands) of students nod off to sleep in my classes. I am reminded of a humbling incident that occurred in one of my First Aid and Safety classes. For that particular class, I encouraged students to participate in class discussion. Since one of the themes of the class was prevention, I felt students could relate some of their experiences that resulted in accidents. The premise was that the whole class could benefit from everybody else's experiences. One particular male student stood out in my memory. Since he was tall and he sat in the middle of the class, I was aware of his presence. As the term progressed, I noted that he never participated in class discussion. I was talking about some topic during the sixteenth week of the term. I was on a roll about something. He raised his hand. As I was completing a response to a question, I was thinking how great this event was. Everyone else in the class had made several contributions to class discussion throughout the sixteen weeks, but he had never said a word. It took sixteen weeks, but he was finally going to participate in class discussion. I thought to myself that this event represented one of the rewarding moments of teaching. So, I finished the point I was making and called on him. He said, "Mr. Kenworthy, you have an ink stain on your shirt pocket. I think that your pen is leaking."

In summary, my teaching experiences were rewarding. I am confident that my teaching left an impact on many people.

ENDORPHIN THERAPY

I ran races (5K's, 10K's, half-marathons, and marathons) for five decades, always in the back of the pack.

A FITNESS ADVOCATE once described the mental and emotional benefits of participating in endurance exercise. He said that he and his wife were arguing about something, and he was stressed by their disagreement. He went out for a three-mile run. After the first mile, he forgot what they were arguing about. After the second mile, he forgot his wife's first name. After the third mile, he forgot how to get home.

As a high school basketball player for Coach West in Guantanamo Bay, I had memories of finishing a practice with "wind sprints" and the resultant feeling of being totally exhausted and euphoric. When I was overcome by the stresses of college living at UF, I would take time to go for a one or two mile run. The result was that my worries and stresses were lessened after the run. Scientists have more recently suspected that this euphoric outcome is possibly attributed to our brain releasing substances called "endorphins." The release of these endorphins is triggered by long and high levels of exercise, causing a dulling of the pain and discomfort from this intense exercise. This phenomenon is known to make you happier. It is also referred to as a "runner's high," and scientists liken the increased production of these endorphins to the feeling that a person gets when he is taking morphine. Some experts argue that in some people, achieving this "runners high" can be addictive.

I suspect that I am an exercise addict. While I am not a fast runner, I have participated in countless races from 5 kilometers (3.1 miles) to marathons (26.2 miles) over a period of five decades. I have never come close to ever winning a race, and I don't remember ever receiving an age-group award. I entered these races for the camaraderie and for that spent and euphoric feeling at the end of the race. Distance running also is a calorie-burner, which I required, since I had a voracious appetite for most of my life.

In the early 1970's, distance running was beginning to gain in popularity. I was part of a small group of fledgling runners who decided to create a local running club for Brevard County. I became a charter member of the "Space Coast Runners." Our mission was to promote running in the county and organize some local running races. While organizing road races today is pretty sophisticated with microchip and GPS technology, our techniques were pretty crude in the 1970's. Runners were less knowledgeable and experienced. I can remember a 6.2 mile race held in Melbourne Beach in late-May that began at 10 a.m. For those not familiar with Florida weather, the high temperature and humidity make a 10 a.m. starting time very dangerous for heat emergencies like heat exhaustion and heat stroke (and death). Recommended starting time would be 7 or 8 a.m. In Florida late May 10-kilometer races are not advised either. November through April is safer. The result was almost suicidal. Local emergency medical personnel were strained, hauling one runner after another to the emergency room. Fortunately, no one died, and lessons were learned.

There was a 10-kilometer race organized in Merritt Island in the early years. The inexperienced and careless race director (not me) measured the course with a damaged measuring wheel. The wheel was one yard in circumference, and it was supposed to have a pin every 12 inches that would trigger the counter to measure the course. One of the pins was broken, giving an inaccurate measurement of the 6.2-mile course. Unknowing to everyone, the course became a 9.3-mile race. The runners were complaining about the excessive distance of the race and really hurting. Again, no one died, and lessons were learned.

I was the race director for the annual Space Coast Marathon for three years (1979-1981). It was quite a chore, since we also conducted a half-marathon concurrently. This resulted in managing 39.3 miles of course throughout the streets of South Brevard. I had to coordinate with Brevard County officials, four municipalities, Florida East Coast Railroad, and the Coast Guard (two drawbridges over the Indian River) in order to ensure that the races would move safely and smoothly. I had a unique advantage in acquiring volunteers for all the various operational needs in conducting a marathon and half-marathon (registration, water stations, light traffic control, finish line coordination, etc.). The marathon was held on the weekend after Thanksgiving, which was three weeks before the end of the semester at BCC. Many of my BCC students were in absence trouble by that point of the semester, and they could have absences removed by volunteering at the marathon. The students jumped at the opportunity to help.

I attempted to keep the races as organized as possible, and I think I did a pretty good job of doing that with one exception. Traffic was blocked off by law enforcement personnel, and during one of the marathons the traffic pattern prevented members of the South Brevard Baptist Church from getting to church on a Sunday morning. I was in trouble with the Baptists. On the Tuesday after the marathon, I had to meet with the Baptist preacher. The reverend hinted that depriving his flock from attending church on Sunday was a pretty serious sin. I apologized and promised to let him attend the police traffic control meeting before the next year's marathon. I also offered him the opportunity to give the invocation prior to next year's marathon. I trust I was forgiven by the Baptists.

The sixth marathon that I ran was in Ormond Beach, Florida in 1987. In that race I decided to push myself to determine just how fast I could complete a marathon. Maybe it was a subconscious suicide wish (I did have three teenage kids at that time). I ran the first 13 miles with reckless abandon and feeling energized. Somewhere around mile 17, I crashed. I didn't take enough nutrition along the course, and the marathon only had water at the aid stations. I struggled during the last 9 miles. Dying felt like a desirable and viable option. I finished feeling really terrible, vowing never to run another marathon.

Ten years later I was retired from BCC with a lot of time on my hands, when I received a phone call from someone with the Leukemia and Lymphoma Society. They had a nationwide fund raising program called "Team in Training." Members of Team in Training pledge to raise funds for medical research and patient services for people impacted by leukemia and lymphoma-type cancers. In addition to raising funds, team members train to run or walk a marathon (or half-marathon). The amount to be raised was determined by which event they were entering, and L&LS had members doing marathons all over the country and world. Over ninety percent of the members were inexperienced distance runners. One of my former students had recommended me as a marathon training coach. I had a dilemma. Ten years earlier I had convinced myself that running 26.2 miles was unnatural and harmful to the human body, and I would no longer run that distance. I also was a plodding, slow runner. After being told that I was

qualified and the perfect person to be a Team in Training Coach, I reluctantly agreed to give it a try.

**These people inspired me. Mostly "non-athletes," they had
something to prove. They raised funds for the Leukemia
and Lymphoma Society and trained to run or walk a 26.2
mile marathon. I was the coach to over 200 "Team in
Training" participants. This group participated in
the 1998 Anchorage, Alaska Marathon.**

My job as a marathon coach consisted of setting up a 5-month training
plan and conducting "long runs" every other weekend along the streets of
Brevard County. The "long runs" started out at 3 miles during the first
month and progressed to 22 miles by the fifth month. The coach also set
up water and Gatorade every 2 miles along the course—a glorified water
boy. The coach also organized seminars on a variety of marathon-related
topics—marathon training principles, injury prevention and treatment, shoe
selection, foot care, nutrition, the mental aspects of running or walking a
marathon. Since over 90% of the runners/walkers were attempting a marathon for the first time, I found myself offering a great amount of advice,
counsel, and encouragement. In the five years that I was a Team in Training
Coach I worked with a few hundred people in the program. I found that
these people were interesting and uplifting. Many of the participants had
family and friends who were impacted in some way by leukemia or lymphoma. Many just wanted to do something for the L&LS cause. Some just

wanted to get into shape, and some liked the idea of traveling. I felt fortunate to be associated with so many positive people and was proud to be part of such an admirable cause. Each member had to raise between $800 and $5,000 for a marathon, depending on the location of the race. While some of the money went toward transportation, hotel, and entry fees, a significant amount of the money raised went directly to research and patient services. As of 2012, the Team in Training program has raised $1.3 billion in 25 years nationwide.

The experience of observing fledgling marathoners beaming with joy and pride at the victory party held on the evening of each marathon was rewarding for anyone involved with teaching and coaching. Twenty-four hours earlier, they were all shaking in their boots. I guess you can say that I got my "coaching fix" with my Team in Training experience. I also got to travel to San Diego, California; Anchorage, Alaska; Disney World in Florida; Helena, Montana; Bermuda; and Dublin, Ireland. But, the greatest benefit was to be associated with so many inspiring people. Many team members became addicted to marathon running and are still doing marathons, while some shared the feeling of one of the team members. He told me, upon finishing a Disney World Marathon, "I just completed two marathons in one day—my first one and my last one." **Barry and Michele Birdwell** succeeded me as Team in Training coaches and have been coaching dedicated people for over a decade. Barry had a family member impacted by a blood cancer. I respect their dedication to the fight against leukemia and lymphoma. I also respect their support to so many novice runners and walkers, who never expected that they would ever do anything like run or walk a marathon.

In addition to distance running, I have played an abundance of handball over four decades. Handball is a very physically demanding game (a good endorphin producer). It can be played on a variety of courts: one-wall, three-wall, or fully enclosed four-wall courts. The courts are 40 feet long and 20 feet wide. The game may be described best as similar to racquetball without the racket. Instead of the racket, you hit the ball with your hands—both hands. One of the primary strategies is to force your opponent to use his less dominant hand often. Handball was invented before racquetball. Historically, various civilizations played forms of the game, but it was most popular in Ireland and brought to the U.S. by the Irish. In this country it was played initially in cities with building walls used as handball courts. I was introduced to it, when I enrolled at the University of Florida. Handball was especially popular in the early 1960's. There were about 30 three-wall courts at the time, and they were in great demand. Handball classes used the courts for much of the morning and early afternoon hours, and students used them recreationally into the night (they were lighted). As a college student, I didn't play much handball; I started playing it in the early 1970's.

Handball is referred to as "the perfect game." Played with a ball and one, three, or four walls, handball has provided me with physical exercise and stress relief for decades. Many of my best friends are handball players.

Exercise physiology textbooks ranked handball as one of the most aerobically demanding activities. They would rank it as a great calorie burning activity. Jogging also was considered a big calorie burner. Since I was aware of how much I enjoyed eating, I decided that handball and jogging would be my two primary physical fitness activities. Socially, I have met some fun and interesting people on the handball court. Part of the fun of handball was the bantering and playful exchanging of insults. Over the four-plus decades of handball playing, when I was sidelined from time to time with orthopedic injuries, I couldn't wait to get back on the court. Baseball playing and distance running caused me to have some discomfort in the shoulders and the knees, but I played through the pain if I could. If I were to make a list of some things that would contribute to my "perfect life," pain-free handball would be near the top of that list. I would often feel that all the planets were aligned, as long as I could get my handball fix two or three times a week. Also, walking off the handball court, I would sometimes forget what I was arguing about with Gloria (or even forget her first name).

Jack with other family handball players-grand niece Sally Kenworthy and son Russ Kenworthy.

BASEBALL UMPIRE

After playing and coaching baseball for many years, I "defected" to the other side of the law by umpiring high school and college games for 28 years.

AFTER 20 YEARS of playing and coaching college baseball, I was realizing an approaching void in the spring of 1981. I was going to miss being on a baseball field, and I was going to miss interacting with many of my friends who were high school and college coaches and professional scouts. Then the idea of umpiring college and high school came to mind. I participated in a three-day baseball umpire clinic, led by then major league umpire, Rich Garcia, and contacted a couple of umpire assigners (**Bill Noland** and **Don Trawick**) for high school and colleges in the Central Florida area and became an umpire.

Umpiring baseball was a strange and different aspect of the game of baseball. As a player and as a coach, there were winners and losers. As an umpire, your goals were to strive for a consistent strike zone and one hundred percent correct calls. The only persons that had your back were your umpire partners. Everybody else would turn on you in a second, if you made a call that was not in their favor. The function of the umpire was to be fair and to maintain and preserve the dignity of the game. I perceived that the expectations of an umpire were lower than those of a player or coach. People regarded umpires as dumb and blind. Umpires were a convenient target for blame when things weren't going well for a team. But, on the plus side, I was back on the baseball field with many of my friends and acquaintances. I didn't have to worry about preparing the field for a game—or keeping track of foul ball baseballs that needed to be retrieved—or trying to motivate players to perform up to their potential—or a variety of other demands that baseball coaches have to deal with. I liked the idea that I had control over how well I performed as an umpire, and I wasn't depending on a bunch of 19 and 20 year-old ballplayers to determine whether I had a successful day on the baseball field. And, unlike when I played and coached, I now was able to win all the arguments, as an umpire.

While I had my uncontrolled moments as a coach, I generally respected umpires and tried to stress to my players the importance of respecting umpires. In fourteen years as a coach, I was only ejected from a game one time. We were losing by six runs in the late innings at ancient Provost Park in Cocoa, Florida, and I was frustrated. The sub-standard lighting at Provost Park made it especially difficult to see balls hit deep in the outfield. A St. Petersburg Junior College batter hit a long drive to right-center field that I thought bounced over the fence for a ground-rule double. The umpire, **Al Gandolfi** (a friend of mine), called the hit a home run. I came out to Al to protest the call. I happened to have some dimes in my back pocket that were used to pay neighborhood kids for returning foul balls. I took a coin out, gave it to Al, and suggested that he could use it to flip to help him make future decisions. I was gone!

I actually received a quarter from an umpire in the middle of a game once. **Reidy Williams** was umpiring on the bases and made a very close call that was not in our favor. It was one of those situations where I had to discuss the call as a gesture of support for my team; I had to make an appearance, even though I suspected that Reidy got the call right. I went onto the field and explained to Reidy what I saw. Reidy explained to me what he saw. After we discussed the call for another 30 seconds, I changed the subject to complain about putting a quarter in a Southern Bell pay phone two nights before and not getting a dial tone. The phone had eaten my quarter. Reidy was a local supervisor with Southern Bell. He pulled a quarter out of his pocket and gave it to me and said, "Jack, Southern Bell apologizes for your inconvenience." We both struggled to keep a straight face.

While I was only ejected one time, I tried to get thrown out of a game at Manatee Junior College in Bradenton one night. Once again we were losing by six runs in the late innings, and Brevard was playing terribly. We made multiple errors, and my pitchers couldn't throw strikes. We were playing sloppy. Umpire **Jim Turner** made a call not in our favor, and I went out to protest. I said all the things that should have gotten me thrown out of the game, waiting and hoping to get ejected. Jim said, "I know what you're trying to do, Jack. I'm not going to throw you out. If I have to stay through this sloppy game, so do you."

As an umpire, I tried to avoid ejecting players and coaches. I attempted to treat everybody on the field with respect, and players and coaches usually reciprocated. In officiating there is a concept called "preventive officiating." Instead of setting up a player or coach for an ejection, an official can take measures to defuse the situation. I would try to let the coach vent for a short time and speak calmly. "Preventive officiating" would not always work. I was umpiring behind the plate in an important high school district tournament baseball game. With runners in scoring position late in the game, a batter grounded out to the shortstop for the third out. Frustrated, the batter purposely stepped on the heel of the outstretched first baseman. I immediately ejected the player; the rules say to eject him. His coach, **Bob Sweeney**, came out enraged. The ejected player was his best player. I let Bob vent for a while, then said, "Bob, you need to calm down or else." Bob replied, "Or else, what? You gonna throw me out of the game? If you've got the balls, then throw me out." I obliged him, "Okay Bob, you're gone." Ejecting him meant that I had to write an ejection report to the state high school association in Gainesville. One of the reasons I did not eject many players and coaches was that I didn't want to do the follow-up paperwork. At the time I was still teaching at BCC. It was finals week at BCC, and I had many deadlines in the next two days. Now I had to fill out some stupid ejection report. I decided to have some fun with it. Umpires were instructed to give verbatim accounts about what was said on the baseball field, and I did. I then explained in the report that when I left my house before the game I had that part of my anatomy (balls), so I ejected him. That legendary ejection report is still discussed among baseball umpires of the Mid Coast Officials Association two decades later.

Speaking of that part of my anatomy, I once took a foul ball directly to the "family jewels." While umpiring behind the plate, a foul ball was hit down between the legs of the catcher and came up to hit me in a vulnerable location. Even though the athletic cup that I was wearing was well designed to deflect most traumas, this foul ball came up and under—a direct blow to the "cojones." After five minutes of recovery time, I bravely, painfully continued the game. Within twenty-four hours my scrotum was entirely black and blue (I know, too much information). For the next two weeks I was in a fragile, tender condition. I was explaining my injury to an umpire partner and friend, **Dennis McComb**, a few days after it happened. He had a memorable response. He said, "Go to the doctor and ask him to give you something for the pain, but nothing for the swelling."

I felt as if I had a pretty good grasp of the rules of baseball. Whenever a controversy arose on the baseball field, I would make it a point to research the rules to assure that I had made the proper interpretation. Over several years on the baseball field as a player, coach, and an umpire; I became an astute student of the rules of baseball. During my first year of umpiring, I would attempt to explain to fans after the game the proper interpretation of a particular rule. I learned very early in my umpire career that nobody was interested in hearing my observations and insights, if there was controversy. All the fans knew was that they were screwed, that umpires were the reason that they lost, and that umpires are blind and dumb. Sometimes the question of how many legal parents the umpire had would be discussed. For that reason, it was best to disappear quickly after the last out. On one particular night I was umpiring a game at Eau Gallie High School. My son, Russell, came with me to the game. He was 12 years old at the time, and he had some friends that were at the game. The game ended with some controversy, and the home team (Eau Gallie) was on the short end of the controversy. That scenario meant that I needed to get to my vehicle in the parking lot and get out of there quickly. I was umpiring behind the plate that night, and I didn't even take the time to remove my umpire equipment. I got behind the wheel and left the premises. About two miles into my escape, I realized that I had left Russell behind. I had to return to the scene of the crime. Fortunately Russell was waiting for me, and I didn't have to get out of my van to search for him. He jumped in, and we hurried home. On subsequent occasions when Russell came to games that I was umpiring, he was aware that when the game was over, he was to rush to the van.

Baseball fans are known for their comments to the umpires. Many people enjoy harassing and ridiculing the umpire from the stands. While some of their remarks are nasty and acerbic, others are original and humorous. I appreciated them, even if I was the object of their quip. Of all the commentary directed at me over 28 years of umpiring, I thought that the best line came from a Liberty University (Jerry Falwell's religious institution, of all places) fan. From behind the plate, I could hear the fan say, "Hey ump, now I know you're blind. I've seen what your wife looks like." When I told Gloria about that comment, she didn't appreciate it. Wives can't see humor in certain things.

Two of my best coaching friends were **Boyd Coffie** from Rollins College and **Jay Bergman** from the University of Central Florida. We had a good relationship, when I coached; and, later I umpired several of their games. On this particular night in late April, Rollins was hosting UCF in Winter Park, Florida. It had been raining all day, and there was a light, steady drizzle one hour before game time. I was in Boyd Coffie's office with Boyd and Jay. Boyd's office was right behind home plate, and it had a large plexi-glass window overlooking the field. Players from both teams were gathered around their respective dugouts; they were joking and trying to stay entertained while awaiting the decision to play the game or not. Boyd and Jay were going over their remaining game schedules in search of a potential make-up date, if tonight's game was postponed. They were having difficulty finding a common make-up date. Boyd said to Jay, "Look at those guys out there. They are hoping that we get rained out, so that they can party and get laid tonight. Jay, if we call this game off, will you be getting laid tonight?" Jay responded, "Probably not, what about you?" Boyd answered, "Probably not, let's play ball!" The game went on, and it continued to rain all night. The game was sloppy and long in duration. As I stood out on the field soaking wet through the whole ordeal, I thought to myself, "They never asked for my input." Such is the life of an umpire.

Umpiring high school and college baseball for 28 years really did fill the baseball void that I anticipated I would have, when I retired from coaching in 1980. I was able to umpire some high school tournament finals games over the years.

One year (1988) I had the opportunity to umpire in the NCAA Division II national championship in Montgomery, Alabama. I can remember one of those tournament games in Montgomery. We had a cramped umpire dressing room behind the first base dugout under the grandstands of the historic Patterson Field. The local baseball umpire association in Montgomery provided us with a huge iced bucket of beverages (mostly beer) in the tiny dressing room. Jacksonville State University from nearby Jacksonville, Alabama had a team in the national tournament, and they attracted a huge crowd for a game one particular night. Jacksonville State lost that elimination game on a very controversial call at first base to end the game. The call was made by the first base umpire, and television film footage later indicated that he got the call right. The J.S.U. fans, coaches, and players went ballistic. In that particular game I was the third base umpire (as far away from that tiny dressing room as you could get). The correct call was made, and all of my umpire partners were running full speed for the dressing room. Fans, coaches, and players were converging on that dressing room. I was the last umpire to reach the dressing room, and I frantically appealed to my fellow umpires to let me in. They let me in and quickly slammed the door to keep the angry crowd from getting to us. We could hear people banging on the door trying to get to us. The dressing room was so tiny and ill-equipped that we hadn't even planned to shower and change there. We planned to do that back at the hotel. We couldn't leave that room, for fear of our life and limb. All we could do was drink the beer provided to us and wait for the angry crowd to subside. An hour later (and several beers later) we were able to safely leave the dressing room and return to the hotel.

Over those 28 years, I had the opportunity to be on the baseball field with dozens of high school and college players, who would ultimately become major leaguers. I was one of the first to witness a University of Michigan freshman legend pitch in his first college game—Jim Abbott, who had a severely withered right arm and essentially pitched and played the game with his left arm only. He pitched several years as a major leaguer. Other future major leaguers (just to name a few) that I had the opportunity to see on the field early in their baseball careers were: Tino Martinez, Craig Biggio, Tim Wakefield, Chipper Jones, and Zack Grienke. Most importantly, umpiring kept me in touch with lots of young baseball athletes and in the loop with my large network of baseball friends and acquaintances.

CHAIR DUTIES

DURING MY LAST few years at Brevard Community College, I had an opportunity to become slightly more important by becoming an academic department chairman. I oversaw the physical education, health, dance, social sciences, and psychology disciplines with a primary responsibility of facilitating the dozens of part-time instructors that taught in those fields. In our department, over two-thirds of our class sections were taught by adjunct faculty (an obvious budgetary strategy). My motivation to be a department chair was solely dictated by the additional pay I would receive. I was not doing the chairmanship gig particularly for the prestige or ego boost. I had made a career decision several years earlier to remain at BCC to work two or three layers below my "Peter Principle" level of incompetence. A 1969 book entitled The Peter Principle by Lawrence J. Peter and Raymond Hull was based on the premise that members of an organization where promotion is based on achievement, success, and merit will eventually be promoted beyond and above their level of ability. I consciously chose to minimize stress in my life by doing things I felt comfortable doing, rather than aggressively striving to improve myself in the college's hierarchy. My Florida state pension benefits were based on the last few years' salary. The additional stipend from being a department chair enabled me to increase my future pension amount, and it did.

My educational leadership philosophy was that teachers (professors) were on the front lines of the teaching/learning process, and that the administrator's function was to serve and support the faculty. Many of my administrators over the years of teaching were not all necessarily supportive to the faculty. I found many of them condescending and resistant toward faculty members, establishing roadblocks to an effective teaching environment. I think many members of our faculty appreciated my supportive attitude toward them. While I wasn't pursuing power or relishing my authority in my duties as a department chair, I did take advantage of one aspect of leadership—controlling the length of faculty department meetings. I hate to count the hundreds (maybe thousands) of hours I had spent in faculty meetings over the years as a faculty member. Very little was accomplished in those meetings, making them a waste of time for most faculty members. Since I was in charge of conducting a monthly faculty meeting, I made the agendas efficient and succinct, rarely lasting longer than twenty or thirty minutes. Faculty meeting attendance was an issue at first; but, I jokingly let it be known that if you were absent from a faculty meeting, we would put you on the agenda and discuss you without your ability to defend yourself. I was only joking, but attendance improved dramatically.

BCC offered a few dance classes each term—ballet, modern dance, jazz dance. I approached the Humanities Department Chair to suggest that the dance discipline be a part of his department, not mine. For some reason, he did not want to oversee dance. While our dance instructors were delightful to know, they were head-strong, proud, individualistic, creative artists (maybe that is why department chairs didn't want to include dance in their departments). On a few occasions, I had to resolve disagreements among the dance faculty. I appreciate interacting with all types of people, and having an opportunity to work with the dance faculty was a challenging, enjoyable, and exhilarating experience.

One year the dance faculty wanted to have an end-of-term dance recital, and I helped to arrange all the logistics for having this event. It was held in the experimental theater of the King Center for the Performing Arts on the Melbourne Campus. It was a well-received event with a couple hundred people in attendance, but not without potential controversy. I was aware that there were a few exotic dancers from some of our local strip clubs enrolled in our dance classes. They were taking dance classes to refine some of their dance moves. Since one of BCC's missions was to enhance and improve the employable skills of the citizens of Brevard County, it could be argued that our dance classes were meeting the college's objectives. The recital included the full spectrum of talent. Some of the students had extensive backgrounds in dance, while some were not very talented. When one of the strippers did her routine, she started shedding some of her clothing, resembling some routine you might see in her place of employment (a strip club). Tension was building inside me, because I wasn't sure when she was going to stop discarding her clothing. I was envisioning that I would be receiving a call from the president's office the next day, demanding an explanation about the content of our dance recital. My pastor was seated next to me. His daughter was performing ballet that night; she was one of the better trained dancers in the recital. During this stripper's routine, I can remember him saying to me, "My, there is an abundance of creativity in this room tonight." She finished her routine still wearing some clothing, and I never received that phone call from the president's office.

I was a chairman in another realm during my last few years at BCC. I was asked to be the state community college baseball committee chairman. There were 27 community college baseball teams in Florida, sub-divided into 4 conferences with a double-elimination state tournament held in May every year. All-State teams were voted on and selected, and an All-Star game with players from teams not qualified for the state tournament was held every year. I coordinated most of these activities. This job was truly a labor of love. I was honored to be asked, and this position kept me in touch with my huge network of baseball friends.

RETIREMENT HONEYMOON

IN THE EARLY 1990's, I was contemplating leaving BCC. I had worked at the same place for 25 years, and the work environment was getting unpleasant. Tensions between faculty and administration were increasingly adversarial and acerbic. Several of my BCC colleagues were having various health issues, and I was convinced that many of these issues were stress-induced. I was ready to bolt. I asked our human resources director to do some numbers for me, if I were to retire from BCC. He reported to me that it would not be in my best interest to leave BCC now (1992), but the numbers looked pretty good in June of 1996. At that time I will have served for 30 years and will be able to collect my pension immediately. I would also receive some other benefits upon separation from BCC. When June of 1996 arrived, Russ was already out of college with a full-time job with benefits. Laci had just earned her bachelor's degree in teaching and was getting married. Shannon had just earned her master's degree. Gloria and I had pretty well completed our parental expectations, and our expenses were not so demanding any longer. I especially remember the satisfied feeling of reducing my auto insurance policy coverage from five cars to two cars. Food expenses and home energy expenses were significantly reduced. I even estimated that our toilet paper expenses had been reduced by 150% (from 5 body openings to 2 body openings). So, I retired in 1996 at the age of 53. The retirement honeymoon began. What a feeling!

I played more golf, and my game improved. I played more handball, and that game improved. I had a steady slate of home projects scheduled. I am not a very talented handyman, but I enjoy and take pride in working on projects around the house. My only two obligations were my two "paying avocations." I had begun umpiring college and high school baseball in 1981 and continued doing that into my retirement. I also continued to keep the official basketball scorebook for Florida Tech, an NCAA Division II college.

In 1985 **Les Hall**, then the baseball coach at Florida Tech, called me to inquire if I knew anyone who would be capable and interested in keeping the official scorebook for the fledgling basketball program that was about to upgrade. Florida Tech had just hired a prominent coach, **Tom Folliard**. Tom had an impressive resume; he had played at Providence College, a reputable basketball program. He had NCAA coaching experience, and he promised to make Florida Tech competitive on the basketball floor. He came from southeastern Massachusetts, not far from my old stomping grounds, Swansea. I was looking forward to attending a few Florida Tech basketball games, since he was bringing in some players from New England. He was also bringing in some New England opponents for the upcoming season. I told Les that I would ask around. A day later I told him I would take the job. I was going to pay to attend some games that year. Why not get paid to watch the games and be in the middle of the action?

I had limited experience scoring basketball, so I had to train myself. I liked the mental stimulation of keeping track of goals scored, fouls committed, time-outs, and recording the game time of all those events. Basketball is a fast-paced game. I was mentally drained after doing two games in one evening (there would often be a women's game followed by a men's game). I look forward to each basketball season, and I hope to continue scoring basketball for many years to come.

My retirement honeymoon included playing handball, playing golf, working on projects around the house, umpiring baseball games, and scoring basketball games. I was enjoying my lifestyle. Gloria was still teaching full-time. Jim Weeks told me that I was his hero, since I was retired with my wife still working.

Gloria was teaching the fifth grade at Sabal Elementary School during my retirement honeymoon. In her early years of teaching, she taught second grade. She took an 18-year hiatus from teaching, raising kids. She let her teaching certificate lapse during this time. In the middle 1980's, we determined that we could no longer survive paying our monthly bills without a second income. Gloria took some college courses to restore her teaching certificate, so she could resume teaching. She took an additional two courses to get a specialized "early childhood education" certification. She rationalized that the extra certification would increase her marketability in securing a teaching job, which she desperately needed. She was hired at Sabal to teach sixth grade, and she grew to enjoy that grade level. She taught either the fifth or sixth grade for several years and enjoyed that age group.

To set up this story, I must mention that when I retired from BCC, I took out a hefty amount of life insurance on my life with Gloria as my beneficiary. It was the least that I could do, since I was now a "slacker retiree." If I died first, Gloria would be compensated fairly. During my retirement honeymoon, Gloria was slated to teach the fifth grade for the upcoming school year. After the first six days of the new school year, Brevard schools conduct an accounting of students who are actually attending school. If schools are above or below expected attendance numbers, adjustments are made by re-assigning faculty to where the student population dictates. Sabal Elementary School attendance was below predictions, so two teachers needed to be transferred from Sabal to another Brevard County school. Generally, the most recently hired teachers were slated to be transferred. At Sabal the most recently hired teachers were two kindergarten teachers; they were transferred to another school. Gloria's principal went through the faculty files to determine who could fill the two vacant kindergarten positions. He discovered that Gloria was certified in "early childhood education," and transferred Gloria to teach kindergarten. Gloria was not happy. Meanwhile, the "slacker retiree" was planning a trip to Atlanta to see a couple of Atlanta Braves baseball games with a friend. As I was leaving for the airport, I told Gloria that I probably would not call her when I arrived in Atlanta. I said, "If the plane crashes, you will see it on CNN." She replied, "If the plane crashes, I am collecting the insurance money, and I am not going to teach kindergarten." The plane did not crash, and Gloria had a long, grueling school year teaching kindergarten kids. I had a long, grueling year having to live with the irate kindergarten teacher. At the end of the year, Gloria called Tallahassee to inquire if she could get her "early childhood education" certification removed from her records. They said they would remove it for $75. She said, "The check is in the mail."

The end of the twentieth century was dominated by orthopedic surgeries. The wear and tear of playing catcher, playing handball, pitching hundreds of hours of batting practice, and running 5K's, 10K's, half-marathons, and marathons had caught up with my body. The surgeries were on my right shoulder and my left knee, two arthroscopic surgeries at each joint. While the "endorphin therapy" appeared to be beneficial to my mental health and cardiovascular health, it was tearing me up orthopedically. My ideal of pain-free handball and jogging was absent in the late 1990's. My joints actually returned to pain-free status in 2006, when I had a total knee replacement on the left knee. I am sure that things will only get worse with body pain, as I progress into my 70's. As I get older, I attempt to stay physically active. My goals have changed. When I was younger, I exercised so that I could have more cardiovascular endurance, muscular strength, and flexibility. Now I exercise to slow down the deterioration process.

About 15 months into my retirement honeymoon, I began to realize that I missed being around lots of people. Working at BCC, I was in social contact with hundreds of people daily. As a retiree, I felt that I was out of the loop socially. I chose to inquire about working part-time at a hospital-based fitness center—Pro Health and Fitness. My son, Russ, had worked there a few years before. That job was Russell's first employment out of college. Laci had worked at the front desk there. I already knew most of the people in management at Pro Health. About the time that I was coerced into becoming a marathon coach with the aforementioned Leukemia Society's "Team in Training," I was hired to work 20 hours a week at Pro Health and Fitness as an exercise floor staff member. My life became very busy again.

PRO HEALTH AND FITNESS

PRO HEALTH AND Fitness is a hospital-based fitness center, belonging to "Health First," which is a network of hospitals, physicians, medical services, and health insurance in Brevard County. Health First operates four different fitness centers in Brevard County, and I ultimately worked at three of them. The Melbourne facility and the Merritt Island facility are each around 50,000 square feet in size with swimming pools. They are each visited by members on an average of 1,200 times a day. The Palm Bay facility is around 18,600 square feet in size with an average of 700 visits a day. The newest facility in Viera is 68,000 square feet with two swimming pools and an average of 1,900 visits per day. At this writing, I have worked part-time with minimal responsibilities at Pro Health and Fitness at three of the four facilities for fifteen years. I can remember my initial interview with the human resources department. "Mr. Kenworthy, how long do you see yourself working at Health First?" My answer was, "Somewhere between ten days and twenty years; I really don't know what I am getting into."

As a floor staff member, my primary job description was to conduct orientations to new members and to roam throughout the exercise floor, assisting members with their exercise programs. Many of the clientele are senior citizens, who are unfamiliar with exercise machines and intimidated by them. I suspected that they felt more comfortable asking me for assistance, since I was closer to their age with wrinkles and thinning grey hair. I thoroughly enjoy this work, although it does not feel like work; I am in my element. A predominance of the members do not look forward to visiting the fitness center. They know that they should exercise regularly, but they do not look forward to the discomfort and pain that often accompanies exercise. I try to be a sociable, friendly, and positive presence in the gym to make their exercise experience tolerable. Most people detest having to go to the gym, but they feel good about themselves when they leave. That clock on the treadmill, bicycle, or elliptical machine can move very slowly while exercising. While some of the members do not want to be bothered, many of them appreciate my "shooting the breeze" with them. I define my job description as "wandering the exercise floor aimlessly, being accessible to the members and conducting bull sessions." I trust and hope that that job description falls within the scope of Health First's expectations of my job performance.

Over the years at Pro Health and Fitness, I have crossed paths with numerous former BCC students and players, BCC faculty and staff, parents and grandparents of former BCC students and players. Pro Health and Fitness records around 1.4 million visits annually at all four centers in Brevard County. Remember, I taught and coached at BCC a total of 30 years—actually I taught and coached for a total of 94 semesters, if you count the condensed summer terms. I know a lot of people in Brevard County. I run across someone that I have not seen in years almost every day that I work at Pro Health and Fitness. For thirty years, I interacted with 18 to 20 year-old students. Pro Health and Fitness members range in age from 18 to 90-plus. One notable difference between the two clienteles is the use of bandages. At BCC, if someone was wearing a bandage of some kind, he had probably been in a fight the night before. A Pro Health and Fitness member wearing a bandage usually means that he or she had recently been to the dermatologist.

My son, Russell, worked on the exercise floor at the Melbourne Pro Health and Fitness a few years before I began my fitness center stint and was a popular worker there. Some of the members recognized my last name and asked if I was related to Russell. Many of them jokingly referred to me as "Russell, Junior."

One memorable experience that I had at the Melbourne fitness center occurred at the swimming pool. I was standing near the door to the pool when three women came out of that door with stressful and disturbing looks on their faces. "You need to go in there and do something about this," they said. I entered the pool area without knowing what to expect. There was only one person in the pool, an elderly gentleman. Upon closer observation, I realized that he was naked. He was confused and embarrassed, when I informed him that he needed to wear a bathing suit. I can only surmise that in his confused state, he may have had recollections of the YMCA or Boys' Club swimming pools 60 or 70 years ago (he looked to be in his eighties). Back then, only males were in the gym, and all the boys skinny-dipped. The justification for kids swimming naked back then was that loose fragments from the fabric of bathing suits would clog the pool filters.

One time at the Melbourne Pro Health and Fitness I had to dart across the exercise floor to respond to a potentially fatal situation. An older husband and wife were trying to analyze how to use a particular exercise machine. The exercise equipment was a Nautilus multi-exercise machine. It featured parallel bars to do an exercise called a parallel bar dip and a chin-up bar with a couple of steps in order to climb up to reach the bars. There were two wrist straps hanging from the chin-up bar that allowed members to do a variety of exercises from the bar. The husband was studying the machine to determine how to use it. He surmised that perhaps the multi-exercise machine could be used as some sort of neck exercise, and he proceeded to convince his wife to step up the steps in order to place one of those straps hanging from the chin-up bar around her neck. The scenario resembled hanging gallows. A co-worker and I frantically arrived in time to rescue the wife. I am pretty sure that the husband did not mean to harm (or hang) his wife, but my cynical mentality considered that perhaps the husband was looking for a way to eliminate his spouse. Additionally, he could sue Nautilus and Health First for liability to make the endeavor profitable.

An eighty-plus year-old lady really shocked me one time. The seats of several of our exercise bicycles were in need of replacement at the Merritt Island fitness center. A few days after they were replaced, I walked by the bicycle section to notice this elderly lady with a very demonstrative, smiling face. She told me, "I really like these new bicycle seats; I think I'm going to have an orgasm." I wasn't prepared for that, and I am sure I blushed. When I told my manager, **Mark Mellen**, later about the incident, he had a good comeback. "You tell her, if she is doing that with our exercise equipment, we are going to have to charge her extra." Word spread among the Pro Health employees about this incident. For a couple of weeks many of the female staff were seen coming out to the workout area to inspect the new bicycle seats.

I worked at the Melbourne Pro Health and Fitness for six months. After six months, Pro Health and Fitness opened a facility on Merritt Island, and I decided that I wanted to go where the new toys were. I knew a few of the members at Merritt Island, having lived there for my first ten years in Brevard County and working at the nearby Cocoa Campus of BCC for six years. Shortly after the Merritt Island facility opened in 1998, a fitness club that had dominated the fitness industry in Merritt Island went out of business. A large amount of members from this failed club migrated to Pro Health, along with some of the working staff members from that club. One of those workers was an elderly guy named **John Robinson**—maybe 76 years old at the time. Several of the new members who migrated from the other fitness club raved about John. They advised our management that John should be hired, and that he would be responsible for many people transferring their membership to Pro Health. He was promptly hired. Members loved him. He was pleasant and was always willing to help anyone interested in strength training and body building. He had a background in body building. While I mentioned that he was always willing to help members, he was especially willing to help the female members. There were rumors that he served as a consultant to some of the ladies to help them determine exactly which size surgical breast implants would look best on them.

When a female would approach John, he would use his trademark line, which was, "You're looking better every day." What female doesn't want to hear that line? They loved him. If he was considered a dirty old man, nobody filed complaints. They all seemed to love him. On occasion, I would hear him suggest to a female member to wear more revealing clothing, so that he could see the "cut" and "muscle definition" of the muscle group that she was working, while she was exercising. Most of the women bought into that concept. John and I would work together as a tandem in entertaining the members on the exercise floor. If he was working with more than one female at a time (which happened often), I would come over and ask John, "Are these ladies holding you against your will?" John's answer was, "I hope so." I would introduce John as being so old that he could remember when the Dead Sea was still just sick.

John was a gentle spirit with a good sense of humor who genuinely loved being around lots of people in the gym—male or female. His two trademark quotes were, "We have a lot of work to do today" and the previously mentioned, "You're looking better every day." He made the members feel good about themselves. He was and still is a legend at the Merritt Island Pro Health and Fitness. He passed away a few years ago, and a small shrine in his memory was installed inside the gym. Years later, members still talk about John.

John Robinson was a popular co-worker at
Pro Health and Fitness.

Another memorable person from Merritt Island Pro Health and Fitness was an old gal named Ruthie. **Ruthie Porter** was about 84, when she first joined Pro Health. She would be first in line when the club opened at 5:30 a.m. Every week day she would participate in the first three or four group exercise classes of the day. She would shower and leave about 11:00 a.m. Then she would allegedly take a nap, drink beer for the duration of her day, go to bed and wake up at 4:00 a.m. to do the same thing all over again the next day. Several female members were relating some of the stories that this old lady was telling in the women's locker room. Many of them were salty and shocking. Ruthie had lived quite a storied life. She was an exotic fan dancer at speakeasies during her younger days. She brought pictures of her dancing days to the club for us to see. She was amazingly sharp, mentally alert, and funny. She related that her nightclub was often raided by local police during her exotic dancing days. She joked that, "To this day when I hear a siren, I reach to put on my underwear."

Ruthie had some other memorable quotes: I saw her in the parking lot one day just before Christmas. I joked with her that she had only two more days to be a good girl for Santa Claus. Her immediate retort was, "I'm not concerned about behaving myself during the days; it's the nights that I worry about." She really made me blush one day, when she gave me a line that she probably used during her nightclub dancing days. As she was leaving the fitness center, she approached me to say, "If I have left you with any hard feelings today, I hope that they are between your legs and not in your head."

Ruthie followed her extremely active regimen of three or four exercise classes a day well into her ninety-fifth year, when she tripped over a curb one day and broke a couple of bones. Her health went downhill quickly. One of our gym members was a volunteer at the local hospital emergency room and was perhaps one of the last people to see Ruthie alive. He said that she did not look too good in the ER, as she sat in a wheelchair. Vince recounted that in spite of her deteriorated condition, she winked at him and said, "Come over and see me some time; you know I'm too old to get pregnant." I continue to miss Ruthie and all of her humorous quips.

I liken all of the social interaction that I experience at the gym to that which you experience at a barber shop or a bar. We could discuss sports, current events, and just about anything except for politics and religion. I would make it a point to divert the conversation, when politics or religion was discussed. I am a modest guy with a number of limitations, but I believe that one of my personal strengths is my ability to conduct a good bull session. If I had something going on in my life, I could share it with the members. If they were on a treadmill, bicycle, or elliptical machine; they were interested in anything that I had to say (they were bored, and the clock was moving too slowly without some diversion).

I can remember one discussion with a club member. A few years ago, I decided to get myself a pre-paid funeral. (I hope that the funeral home doesn't go out of business, and all the funeral bills get covered, but I won't be around to worry about it). Since pre-paid funerals would make a good topic for a bull session, I shared my story with one of the members who was walking on a treadmill. I told him, "I had the strangest experience yesterday. I was seated at my dining room table with my wife and another woman, and we were discussing my funeral plans." The member responded, "And today they are meeting without you to determine when and how you die."

Two of my hundreds (probably thousands) of friends at the gym were **Herm and Marge**. Herm had memory issues. At first I thought that Herm was faking dementia, since Marge had given him hell for forgetting their anniversary date, and he needed an excuse for the oversight. Ultimately, Herm was diagnosed with some form of dementia. Marge was a good wife. She persistently ensured that Herm got some regular exercise at the gym a few times a week. Marge also persistently insisted that I keep an eye on Herm to make sure that he was not slacking off with his exercise routine. Herm was known to set the treadmill at the lowest possible speed, when Marge was not around. One day I noticed Herm walking extremely slowly on the treadmill. I informed him, "Herm, you are going to have to go faster on the treadmill. If you don't, Marge is going to come over and get mad at both of us. Now, I only have to deal with Marge a couple of times a week. You have to deal with her all the time." Herm replied, "Want to switch places?"

At the Merritt Island Pro Health there were a few exercise bicycles directly behind and facing some treadmills. One day a scantily-clad young female was jogging on one of the treadmills. Directly behind her was an old guy on a bicycle, taking in the sights. The girl had been on the treadmill about twenty-five minutes, when I noticed the old guy motioning for me to come see him. He informed me, "You'd better keep an eye on me. I have never been on this bicycle this long before, but as long she is running, I'm staying here."

I didn't know the perpetrator, but one incident at the club stood out in my memory. One of the many duties of a floor staff employee at Pro

Health is to periodically walk through the locker room and restrooms to make sure everything is in order and clean. One day I came upon a toilet with a huge mass of fecal matter (turd) in the bowl, probably the longest intact fecal mass (turd) that I had ever seen. As I went to flush the toilet, I noticed that someone had written a note on the handle, "Do not flush— record pending." I broke out in laughter and honored the request. It was too funny to destroy that scene. (Sorry for the bathroom humor).

After ten years at the Merritt Island facility, I transferred to a new Pro Health and Fitness facility in a new developed community called Viera. Again, my reason for transferring to Viera was that I wanted to go where the new toys were. The Viera facility can best be described as tasteful and palatial with an abundance of exercise equipment and facilities. Moving to the new facility enabled me to meet even more friends. I continue to enjoy my part-time status at the gym with limited responsibilities. When I told the human resources person in 1997 that I saw myself working at Pro Health and Fitness somewhere between 10 days and 20 years, I initially expected that my tenure would be closer to 10 days. I have been doing this Pro Health gig for over 15 years. I have enjoyed being in the healthy and active environment that you find at a hospital-based fitness facility. I have enjoyed being around all the interesting old people and the good-looking young people.

CABIN IN THE MOUNTAINS

LACI AND DEAN lived in southwest Virginia, a pretty area along the Blue Ridge Mountains with an abundance of woods, mountains, and beautiful views. Since they were the only ones who had provided us with a grandchild (Jenna) for a long period of time, we spent more time visiting them than we did visiting Russ and Shannon. During the visits, I would look at real estate magazines for potential property in the area. On occasion, I would let realtors take me to some sites. In the back of my mind, a perfect property would be somewhat secluded and wooded on the side of a mountain with a beautiful vista. I couldn't find anything with those criteria for a few years.

Everyone remembers what they were doing and what they were thinking during the terrorist tragedy on September 11, 2001. I was working the exercise floor at the Merritt Island Pro Health and Fitness Center and watching with disbelief the collapsing buildings on television. Three thoughts crossed my mind:

1) I need to get on the handball court, play some handball, and escape reality for a while (remember my aforementioned endorphin therapy).
2) I hope and pray that our national leadership doesn't screw up the United States' response to this attack.
3) I want to have the option to get lost in a cabin on the side of a mountain in southwest Virginia.

I played two hours of handball immediately after my work shift. Many agree that our national leadership was less than stellar in the response to 9/11 (but I don't pursue political discussions). A few months later upon our next visit to see Jenna in Virginia, I looked for those five acres on the side of a mountain more aggressively.

My son-in-law, Dean, took Laci up to the hills of Virginia immediately after their wedding in 1996. He wanted to return to his boyhood home. Laci was a good sport to leave her Florida home, but she adapted well to the lifestyle in the Virginia mountains. The best way to describe the type of friendly people in that area is to recognize that Mount Airy, North Carolina is not far away. Mount Airy is the birthplace of actor Andy Griffith and the inspiration of the fictional television town of Mayberry. Many years before Dean was in the picture, Gloria would mention that her family had connections somewhere in Virginia. Gloria's subsequent genealogy research revealed that her ancestors had settled in the United States in the 18th century near a place called Draper, Virginia. Ironically, Dean's hometown was within a few miles of Draper, Virginia. Guess where we eventually purchased five acres of woods on the side of a mountain—Draper, Virginia. We even came upon a local settlement map from 1838 and found a couple of Fugate settlements that were geographically within six miles of the property that we had purchased in 2003.

I remember Gloria mentioning in earlier decades that she would like to have the experience of building a new home, as opposed to the two pre-owned homes that we had lived in. I called her bluff. Some Fugate inheritance money made it possible, if I could talk her into building a house on those five acres of woods on the side of Draper Mountain. She reluctantly agreed. A new project was launched. The previous owner was selling the property, as a result of his impending divorce. He had a vision of putting a house about one-third of the way up the mountain. The mountain became too steep any higher than that. We adopted his vision, because the view from there looked pretty.

We perused numerous publications of house plans and narrowed our preferences down to five. We found an excavation contractor named **Jeff Worrell** and a general contractor named **Harold P.**

"Cookie" Dalton. After walking through the steep terrain to the desired house location, I showed Jeff and Cookie our five proposed plans. They both agreed that there was only one possible house plan that would fit on the side of the mountain, so we went with that one. The house is a chalet-type structure that includes lots of windows and a wrap-around deck that allows many opportunities to take advantage of the view of mountains and valleys.

Our general contractor, Cookie, is shown here discussing the house plans with Laci (our Virginia liaison person) and me.

Since we had never built a new house before, I read a few books on how to protect myself from unscrupulous contractors. This project was going to be expensive, and we would be 700 miles away in Florida much of the time. I was questioning my wisdom for even undertaking this venture. I was on edge, hoping that the contract that we had signed covered all the bases and protected us from fraud and other dishonest practices. After two months I realized that Jeff and Cookie were men of character and honesty—and conducted their business with a handshake and eye contact. I decided to disregard those books. Jeff was delightful to work with. He could look at the mountainous woods and determine which way the rain-water would flow off the mountain. He knew where to put the driveway and the culvert pipes. All I could see was trees on the side of the mountain.

Cookie was a joy to work with—a strong work ethic with a mischievous and comedic approach toward life. Most importantly, he took great pride in his projects. The only criticism that we heard about Cookie was that he sometimes took a long time to finish, because he treated each house as if he were building his own house and wanted to get it right. His crew consisted of his son, **"Bud,"** and his two grandsons, **Shane** and **John**. They were all amiable people who could easily be characters from Mayberry. Were we ever lucky to select those contractors!

One memory stands out during the construction of our mountain home. Excavator Jeff served all our needs for the house site and the driveway (350 feet long) below the house. While the house was being built, it was determined that the steep mountain behind the house was going to necessitate a huge retaining wall; the house was literally being built into the side of the mountain. Cookie got a quote from someone who could put in a long concrete wall maybe up to 15 feet high behind the house. The price tag was going to be $25,000. Cookie said that he knew someone who might be able to terrace and literally re-shape the mountain above the house for a lot less money. He said that **Maurice** was 64 years old; he had dropped out of school when he was sixteen and had been on a bull dozer six days a week ever since. Maurice came out and said that he could re-shape the mountain and utilize some extra fill to flatten out the driveway. Having been an educator, my first impression was that I was a little wary dealing with a high school dropout. I mentioned to Laci that while I felt reasonably confident with Cookie and Maurice, I thought I would like someone with a college education to take a look at our mountain. One of Laci's teaching colleagues was married to someone who specialized in mountainous site preparations, and she arranged to have him come out to our property to give an assessment. I arranged for this college-educated guy to see our site with Maurice present. They walked and talked up and down the mountain together. After they were finished, I accompanied the college-educated man to his car. I instructed him to send me a bill for his consulting services. He told me, "No charge—and that guy, Maurice, has the equipment, expertise, and experience to re-shape the mountain. You're in good hands."

Our Draper Mountain Getaway.

We received our certificate of occupancy in 2006. The new house has given us a new project to challenge us. For the most part, the project has been rewarding. While it is challenging and expensive, we enjoy the house as a getaway. We still live in Florida most of the year. We enjoyed doing some landscaping around the house for the next few years, until something bad happened.

In May of 2010 we were planting some flowers near the house. Gloria was planting a flower near the top of our 350 foot steep driveway. While putting a shovel into the ground, the shovel hit a rock, and Gloria lost her balance. She began running uncontrollably down the driveway. She ran for about 200 feet before she finally fell, landing on her left shoulder. The diagnosis was a fracture dislocation of the shoulder. The head of the humerus bone was shattered. We went through four surgeries in the next three years, before her range of motion and function were somewhat restored with a reverse shoulder replacement surgery procedure. Gloria had three years of her life completely interrupted by this traumatic accident, resulting in much heartache, headache, and shoulder ache. At this writing, Gloria's mental and emotional outlook is on the mend—along with her shoulder.

RECAP

JACK AND GLORIA live in Melbourne, Florida much of the year, visiting the Virginia mountain getaway some of the time. When we are not getting on each other's nerves, we enjoy visiting our family members, who reside in three different states. We enjoy watching our grandchildren mature. We enjoy our very limited responsibility in raising those five grandchildren. We also feel pride that those grandchildren are fortunate to have such loving and competent parents as Russ, Shannon, and Laci (and their spouses). Maybe you have seen the bumper sticker, "If I had known that grandchildren would have been so much fun, I would have had them first." The sticker that I like is, "Grandchildren are God's gift to you for not killing your own."

Recalling my seventy plus years of living has been a fulfilling and rewarding endeavor. As a youngster, I remember enjoying a 1950's television show entitled "This Is Your Life." In the show, a famous person would be surprised by a show host with various family and friends appearing on the show, recounting memorable moments of his/her past life. Additionally, I have enjoyed reading biographies of renowned personalities. This book is my autobiography, recalling events and acquaintances, unlike those of anyone else on this earth. I don't consider myself being particularly famous, illustrious, prominent, important, distinguished, or renowned. But, as that journalist pointed out to me, **everyone has a story to tell**. Everyone has his own unique experiences and his own group of family, friends, and acquaintances. I hope that you have enjoyed Jack's life along with many of the "People Who Knew Jack."

A VARIETY OF JACK'S REFLECTIONS, INSIGHTS, AND OPINIONS

On Lowering Expectations—

As a coach and teacher, I stressed the importance of setting far-reaching goals and striving to attain those goals. The message was to "be all you can be" or "be better than you really are." While I believe in goal-setting, I have found that if my day did not turn out quite right; I often had to back off, concede, and settle for less. In fact, I am convinced that lowering expectations is perhaps the best way to cope with much of the junk that life throws at you. I sincerely believe that lowering expectations is a primary strategy for combating life's frustrations and achieving happiness. I recommend it. I often utilized my silent mantra, "Lower your expectations, Jack."

On Getting Older—

Our house in Melbourne has always been white with brown trim, and I have painted that house the same colors several times in the last 38 years. In the early years I can remember checking my hair in a mirror after painting, looking for white paint that was inadvertently spattered in my brown hair. I also would use a comb to inspect my hair for any spattered brown paint that may be concealed in my brown hair. Well, you guessed it. About twenty years into my home ownership, the white paint would be concealed in my white hair; the brown paint was now easily visible. That observation was one of the first hints that I was getting older.

I had a nice part-time shift, when I was working at the Merritt Island Pro Health and Fitness Center. I worked from 7 a.m. to 11 a.m. Monday through Friday—20 hours a week. One of my co-workers, **Elizabeth**, informed me one day that she had a dream about me the night before. What guy wouldn't want to hear that an attractive younger woman was dreaming about him? Thinking vain and erotic thoughts, I asked her to tell me all about her dream. She said that actually it was a sad dream. In her dream I had died, and many of the floor staff members were fighting over my 7 to 11 shift (a hint that I was getting older).

I continue to enjoy keeping the official scorebook at Florida Tech. Part of the job consists of assistant coaches approaching the scoring table to confirm various data that I record in the scorebook. One night during a women's game, a young and attractive female assistant coach came to the table to inquire how many time-outs her head coach had remaining. Two minutes later she returned to the table with the same question. She returned to the table for a third time, even though the charged time-out situation for her team had not changed. The guys (mostly older males) at the scoring table were all laughing about it. When I suggested to them that I thought that she was perhaps "hitting on me," **Steve O'Neill**, the clock operator had a sobering retort. "Maybe you remind her of her grandfather, and she misses him" (another hint that I was getting older).

While I am getting older, I have been fortunate to avoid any bad health diagnoses (so far). Many of my friends have not been so lucky, and I continue to ask myself, "Why not me?" I will just go as long as I can, even though I am aware of my mortality. I am reminded of the lyrics of a favorite Irish folk song, "Always remember, the longer you live, the sooner you bloody will die."

On Politics—

I am amazed at how people get so passionate and angry over politics. If I thought that my liberties and rights were jeopardized in a serious way, I would get proactive; but, for now I stay abreast of current events and stay out of political discussions. If I sense people want to share their political agenda with me, I go to the other side of the room.

I am a registered Republican, because Republicans offer more candidates for me to choose in primary elections than Democrats in Florida at this time. I vote for the person, not the party.

I believe that politicians should follow the lead of NASCAR drivers, who wear patches on their clothing to identify their sponsors. We, as citizens, would like to know all the campaign donors that made it possible for a particular politician to win his or her election. Then we could better understand the legislators' motives to vote the way that they do.

On Military Service—

I never served in the military. I have mixed feelings about that. I was inspired by all who served in World War II. I felt that it was my duty to do my part to defend my country and to defend its values. When my time came, we were involved in Vietnam. With the military draft in effect, I had a student deferment and subsequently had deferments for being in education, being married, and being a father. I chose to take advantage of those deferments, since they were accessible to me. I did not participate in peace rallies, but I had a difficult time justifying our involvement in jungles on the other side of the world. If called to serve, I would have gone willingly and with patriotic pride. At the time, Communism was spreading throughout the world (including in the Western Hemisphere). If we had engaged in war closer to home, I would have beaten down the doors of the recruiter's office to enlist. I was making preparations to drop out of the University of Florida to enlist in the military during the Cuban Missile Crisis in October 1962.

I respect all who served in the military during the Vietnam conflict, and I feel a level of remorse that I didn't put myself in harm's way, as they did. I had many friends and acquaintances who served, and many of them were killed or physically, mentally, or emotionally maimed from Vietnam.

On the Rewards of Teaching and Coaching—

It is an established fact that almost all teachers (and coaches) make modest salaries. I can remember struggling to pay bills and sarcastically telling myself that I am doing this for all the rewards of being a teacher and a coach. At the time, I was not appreciating those "rewards." Teachers and coaches do, in fact, impact the lives of many. In my case, I was mostly interacting with 18 to 20 year-old students and players beginning adulthood. Dozens of former students and players have remarked to me in later years their appreciation for something that I did for them or said to them.

Attending funerals of my former teaching and coaching colleagues, I often reflect that the departed person in the casket has left an impact with dozens, hundreds, or even thousands of former charges (students or players). Most teachers can be assured that they left their mark on the lives of many. They can be assured that their life fulfilled a purpose. Not everyone in a casket will have that impact.

I feel that coaching athletes increases the level of influence you have on young people. Participating in athletics is characterized by goal-setting, striving for perfection, experiencing hardships, recovering from setbacks. It also includes maintaining the spirit of teamwork, composure, and pride. Coaches are influential in leading young people through these processes.

We all know that parents and teenagers have difficulty communicating. As a coach, I received more than a few phone calls from perplexed and frustrated parents, asking me to "talk some sense into my boy." As years progressed, and I had stepped down as a baseball coach; I found myself getting on the phone to Russell's high school coach (**Ken Campbell**) appealing to him to "talk some sense into my boy."

On Spirituality—

I was born into an Episcopalian family—aka "a Cradle Episcopalian." I continue to have a level of comfort, celebrating the Holy Eucharist in an Episcopal Church most weeks. While in Guantanamo Bay, we had generic Protestant services with Navy chaplains who may have been Methodist, Presbyterian, Baptist, Lutheran, or whatever. Occasionally, a chaplain with Episcopalian affiliation would visit the naval base, and Lois would express her appreciation of the Holy Eucharist. I didn't care at the time. My main concern was being at church on the Sundays when the transport ship arrived early Sunday morning, and getting a sneak preview of any newly-arrived teenage girls. Wanting to attain Lois' approval in later years, I would send her church bulletins of Episcopal Churches that I had attended.

Serving as a "pledge" at the Theta Chi fraternity in 1962, I was instructed that I was to say the blessing the next night at supper. I was not very adept at public prayer, so I researched the Episcopal Prayer Book for an appropriate and short invocation and then memorized it. I delivered grace the next night. The memorized prayer ended with the words, "for Christ's sake." Depending on the inflection of your voice, "for Christ's sake" can be perceived in a very ecclesiastical, reverent way; or, it can be perceived as a way of urgently emphasizing something in a crude way (as in "FOR CHRIST'S SAKE!!"). My blessing came across in the latter manner. Laughter erupted in the dining room.

Decades later, I was caught off guard at a college umpires meeting in Orlando and asked to deliver an invocation before the meeting started. My invocation consisted of stammering and stuttering. Upon completion of my public prayer, there was laughter. I heard someone say, "Don't quit your day job." I still need to work on my public prayer delivery.

Over my seventy-plus years, I have communicated with God in times of uncertainty or duress. Prayer enables me to have comfort, strength, and courage in stressful situations. I think that I prayed most often, when our kids were teenagers. I have to admit that I continue to have a difficult time trying to figure out God—whom he protects and whose prayers he answers. Bad things happen to good people who just happen to be in the wrong place at the wrong time. Why didn't God protect them? Does God really micro-manage all of our personal experiences? While I have all these doubts, I continue to find comfort and strength in communicating with God. I also try to emulate the life and teachings of Jesus Christ, in hopes that his death represented forgiveness for me. It would have been helpful if Jesus had lived long enough to have teenage kids of his own, so Gloria and I could have had a little more direction as parents. I am also not sure what will happen when I die, but I won't be surprised if St. Peter meets me at the Pearly Gates and says, "Oh, you're the one who was married to Gloria and experienced all her drama first-hand for five decades. Come right in; there is a special place in heaven for you." I love Gloria, but she seems to introduce drama to our life very often.

On My Benign, Light-Hearted Cynicism—

Some people (like Gloria) think that I am not serious enough. I am often looking for evidence of the folly of man, and I find it everywhere. Blame that on Ken and Lois. Human behavior is full of humor and irony. One can argue that joking about human nature is a coping mechanism in dealing with reality. I am guilty as charged. One of my favorite books was released many years ago. The book's title was <u>Don't Sweat the Small Stuff—and it's all small stuff</u> by Richard Carlson. Much of what we humans worry about doesn't amount to a hill of beans. I am accused of being shallow-minded and simplistic. I am also guilty of those charges. My sense of humor could be described as self-deprecating. I refuse to take myself too seriously.

On My Three Favorite Comic Strips in the Newspaper—

Humor that touches on truth and reality is the funniest humor. For that reason, I have three favorite comic strips.

Dilbert portrays co-workers and the workplace environment in a sarcastic and cynical way. When I was in the full-time work force at Brevard Community College, I witnessed the inane, insane, and inhumane manner in which co-workers treated each other. One of my prayers in church every Sunday was an appeal to God to help me deal with the "bastards" in the upcoming week (I have already mentioned my inability to articulate effectively in my prayers; but, I trust that God understood what I was saying). Most of my co-workers and supervisors weren't "bastards" (I liked most of them), but they were forced to act like "bastards" within the organizational structure of the college. My coping mechanism was humor, similar to what you read in Dilbert.

Zits features parents going through all the outrageous and unpredictable struggles of raising a teenager. Looking back, the parenting of teenagers was a wild ride. Many of our friends had much wilder rides than we did. The ride included: guiding them through high school and college, keeping them on the right side of the law, hoping that they would attain a positive and wholesome value system, hoping that they would not place themselves behind too many obstacles that would interfere with success as an adult.

Generally, Gloria and I hoped to produce responsible adults; and, all indications are that we did well. I continue to enjoy Zits, but as a grandparent with limited responsibilities.

Pickles depicts an older "empty-nest" couple often getting on each other's nerves, because they have lived together for several decades. Gloria and I fit that profile. Gloria has a difficult time dealing with my flippant attitude, and I have a difficult time dealing with all the drama that she creates on a daily basis. I sometimes pick up some coping tips from the old man. I don't think Gloria reads the comic strip, but she should. She could pick up some pointers herself from the old lady.

On Quality of Life—

Looking past a few thousand disappointments that I have experienced over seventy years, I still feel fortunate to have lived a good life. I still have enough memory to compose this memoir. Gloria and I are proud of Russ, Shannon, and Laci and their accomplishments. I have hundreds (maybe thousands) of relatives, friends, and acquaintances. At this writing, I have avoided any major ailments. Looking at my future, I am sure that my time is coming.

Everybody has his (or her) definition of "quality of life." Your definition is perhaps different from mine. My definition includes continued love from my family, some mobility, no excessive pain, a somewhat lucid mind, and dignity. I sincerely hope that I can maintain my quality of life right up to the moment of my demise. Getting shot out of the saddle doesn't sound too bad!

Compiling my life experiences in this book was a goal that I undertook two years ago. In summary, the recollection of the many **people who knew Jack** throughout all these years contributed immensely to Jack's quality of life.